The Ultimate Guide to Self-Regulation in the Classroom

OTHER TITLES FROM THE SAME AUTHOR

Getting Your Class to Behave, sixth edition by Sue Cowley

How to Survive Your First Year in Teaching: Fourth edition, fully updated for the Early Career Framework by Sue Cowley

The Ultimate Guide to Adaptive Teaching by Sue Cowley

The Ultimate Guide to Mark Making in the Early Years, second edition by Sue Cowley

The Ultimate Guide to Self-Regulation in the Classroom

Sue Cowley

BLOOMSBURY EDUCATION
LONDON OXFORD NEW YORK NEW DELHI SYDNEY

BLOOMSBURY EDUCATION
Bloomsbury Publishing Plc
50 Bedford Square, London, WC1B 3DP, UK
29 Earlsfort Terrace, Dublin 2, Ireland

BLOOMSBURY, BLOOMSBURY EDUCATION and the Diana logo are trademarks of
Bloomsbury Publishing Plc

First published in Great Britain 2025 by Bloomsbury Publishing Ltd

This edition published in Great Britain 2025 by Bloomsbury Publishing Ltd

Text copyright © Sue Cowley Books Ltd, 2025

Sue Cowley has asserted her right under the Copyright, Designs and Patents Act, 1988, to
be identified as Author of this work

Bloomsbury Publishing Plc does not have any control over, or responsibility for, any
third-party websites referred to or in this book. All internet addresses given in this
book were correct at the time of going to press. The author and publisher regret any
inconvenience caused if addresses have changed or sites have ceased to exist,
but can accept no responsibility for any such changes

All rights reserved. No part of this publication may be reproduced or transmitted in any
form or by any means, electronic or mechanical, including photocopying, recording, or any
information storage or retrieval system, without prior permission in
writing from the publishers

A catalogue record for this book is available from the British Library

ISBN: PB: 978-1-8019-9528-3; ePDF: 978-1-8019-9529-0; ePub: 978-1-8019-9526-9

2 4 6 8 10 9 7 5 3 1 (paperback)

Typeset by Newgen KnowledgeWorks Pvt. Ltd., Chennai, India
Printed and bound in the UK by CPI Group Ltd, CR0 4YY

To find out more about our authors and books visit www.bloomsbury.com
and sign up for our newsletters

Contents

Acknowledgements vi
Foreword by *Dr Naomi Fisher* vii

Introduction 1

Part One An Introduction to Self-Regulation

1   The Importance of Self-Regulation and Metacognition 7

2   Self-Regulation: What It Is and How It Develops 19

3   Behaviour as Communication: From Co-Regulation to Self-Regulation 35

Part Two Supporting the Development of Self-Regulation in the Classroom

4   Managing My Behaviours 47

5   Developing Impulse Control and Delayed Gratification 65

6   Building Focus and Attentional Control 79

7   Developing Emotional Self-Regulation 97

8   Supporting the Development of Empathy 117

9   Goal Setting, Resilience and Agency 129

Conclusion 147

Further Reading 149
References 151
Index 157

Acknowledgements

Thank you to the team at my publishers, Bloomsbury, for their support and assistance with creating this book, especially Emily Evans. Thanks to all the colleagues and children, past and present, with whom I have worked over the years, for everything they have contributed to my thinking on this subject. And special thanks, as always, to all my family, my mum and especially to Tilak, Álvie and Rui.

Foreword

There's a contradiction at the heart of how we manage children's behaviour.

For surely what adults want for children is for them to grow into people who can make choices for themselves. People who behave themselves not because they are afraid of the consequences if they don't, but because they want to do well. People who do not require constant supervision because they are self-motivated and can think for themselves. People who can manage themselves and their emotions.

We want, in other words, for them to become autonomous, self-regulated human beings. We want them to grow into people who can be trusted to do the right thing, even when no one is watching.

And yet, much current behaviour management advice for teachers does not hold this goal in mind. Instead, 'behaviour management' can sometimes be a euphemism for 'control'. Children's behaviour is controlled by adults, with varying degrees of success. If they don't comply, there are sanctions, whilst if they do comply, they get rewards and approval. There's little potential for practising autonomy there.

Sue Cowley is someone who understands this contradiction better than most. That's not just because of her years of experience in education, it's because of how varied that experience is. She's taught in primary and secondary schools, and has led and taught in an Early Years setting. She has gained a bird's eye view on the differing priorities of the different stages of education and child development, and how these connect up (or don't).

In Early Years, as Sue points out, the skills of self-regulation are a priority. Developing agency and independence are essential skills for young children. In a good Early Years setting, learning how to be yourself in the world is as important as any formal work. Behaviour isn't seen as something to be controlled by adults so children can learn. Self-regulation of behaviour *is* what children are learning.

As children get older, however, the focus of the education system shifts towards the formal curriculum. Promoting self-regulation is no longer an explicit priority, and consequently, it falls off the radar. Behaviour starts to be seen as a barrier to learning, rather than a fundamental part of education.

Learning how to manage yourself in the world isn't done by age five, however. In fact, it's only just beginning, and neuroscientific research indicates that young people are still developing the skills of self-regulation up to the age of 25 and beyond. This doesn't happen in a vacuum. The development of self-regulation is experience-dependent. At some point, children will make their own choices, and practising doing this in a safe environment is an essential part of growing up. Even if their choices aren't always what adults would have chosen for them.

Unfortunately, as Sue discusses, the research shows that some commonly used behaviour management techniques can actually prevent children from developing the skills of self-regulation. The more adults take control, the fewer opportunities there are for children to practise doing so. Silent corridors may be efficient, but they aren't quiet because the children have learnt to self-regulate. They're quiet because they fear the consequences of making a noise. The research shows that they are unlikely to continue to walk quietly when the supervision ends. In fact, they may be less motivated to do so than they were before the consequences were put in place. The tools which enable us to control children may work in the short term, but they don't help children learn how to control themselves. The skills of self-control and being controlled are different.

But it's also true that classrooms and schools cannot function without a certain level of behavioural control. Just letting children do whatever they want isn't an option. So how can teachers manage behaviour in a way which fosters self-regulation, whilst ensuring that their classroom is a calm learning environment for all?

That's what Sue brilliantly explains in her book. She starts with self-regulation and self-determination theory and shows why the methods which many reach for when managing children's behaviour can have a downside. She talks us through the ways in which children are developing and how behaviour reflects their developing skills of self-regulation. She tackles the 'behaviour is communication' debate head-on. She teases apart many of the different ways in which children learn to self-regulate – including impulse control, attention, goal setting and emotions, and she traces the way that these skills are learnt – through real-life practice and modelling by adults.

There's lots to take in, but the book is eminently readable and practical. Sue doesn't just explain the theory, she provides ideas as to how teachers can support children to learn those skills in the classroom – as well as how to manage behaviour in a way which plays to children's strengths. From the first chapter, there are suggestions as to what teachers can do to help children develop the skills they will need, whilst also managing their class effectively. Her suggestions are imaginative, down-to-earth and immediately applicable. She is realistic about what is possible in a classroom, whilst never losing sight of the end goal – young people who can regulate their own behaviour and learning.

This is a book filled with lightbulb moments. If you've ever wondered how to balance managing your class's behaviour with supporting them to develop the self-regulatory skills they'll need for the future, then this is the book for you.

Dr Naomi Fisher

Clinical Psychologist specialising in autism, trauma and alternative education.

Author of *Changing Our Minds: How Children Can Take Control of Their Own Learning* and *A Different Way to Learn: Neurodiversity and Self-Directed Learning.*

Introduction

The topic of behaviour is a key one for educators: 'How can I get my class to behave so that learning can take place?' Although we tend to think about behaviour in terms of systems and strategies, behaviour is actually part and parcel of a bigger picture around learning. The 'subject' of behaviour encompasses a range of skills that children and young people need to learn in order to be successful in school and beyond. As well as learning 'a curriculum' when they are with us, children and young people are also learning *how to behave* or, in other words, how to self-regulate. The development of self-regulation appears as a key learning goal within the Early Years Foundation Stage (EYFS) in England, and in other curricula internationally as well. How can we build an approach and a curriculum that supports 'learning to behave' within the education system – one that embeds self-regulation within the daily lives of our schools? That is the question that this book sets out to answer.

A brief glance at the Education Endowment Foundation (EEF) website shows that there is a great deal of research to demonstrate why self-regulation is one of the most important skills for children and young people to develop, and how this supports positive long-term outcomes in their education. And yet, it is a relatively under-explored aspect of the learning that happens in schools and settings. This book is designed to give you an introduction to and overview of the subject and to give you plenty of practical examples of what we can do in our settings to support children to learn this vital set of skills. Part One of the book gives you an introductory overview of the subject as a whole – what self-regulation is, why it is important and how it develops. Part Two of the book dives into the specific details about how to support children and young people in the range of self-regulation skills that they are developing, with plenty of strategies to use in your classroom. As with all my books, the focus is very much on a practical approach, sharing up-to-date information on the topic alongside realistic ideas that busy teachers and leaders can incorporate to make their teaching, their classroom management and their schools more effective. This book will also give you an insight into what the latest research says about this fascinating aspect of children and young people's development. As educators, our goal is that our learners understand 'how to behave' in the widest sense, so that when they finish their formal education they can participate in society as fully-rounded individuals.

When we talk about 'managing behaviour' in schools, we often focus on how we can create systems that will manage off-task or challenging behaviours. In turn, we create school policies that start with a set of rules, and these are then reinforced by using rewards, sanctions and interventions that gradually increase in seriousness. While these behaviourist approaches can be useful, it is important to think more widely about what we mean by 'behaviour'. We can view it as part of what children and young people are *learning to do* in schools – the skills that we want them to develop. The term 'self-regulation' encompasses many aspects of behaviour, including:

- emotional regulation
- attentional control
- goal setting
- building a sense of responsibility and empathy
- encouraging impulse control.

When we look at behaviour through the lens of how children learn and develop, we can think more fully about what we can do as teachers to support this process. We can also start to widen our focus, away from using solely behaviourist systems to control and manage classrooms, and towards teaching learners to make better and more conscious decisions about their behaviour.

We live in an increasingly complex and challenging world, and the pandemic has led to what many teachers describe as an increase in problematic behaviours. In the Early Years setting that I help to run, we have certainly seen children coming to us with elevated levels of need, especially around self-regulatory behaviours. During my work with education colleagues around the world, I hear about the issues that children and young people are experiencing with social communication, resilience, coping with failure and managing emotions – all aspects of self-regulation. By considering the question 'What skills do they need to learn?', we should be able to help our children and young people to deal more effectively with the difficulties that we and they currently face.

Since writing my first book on behaviour almost 25 years ago, I have developed a fascination for the subject. I have gradually expanded my interest in 'managing' behaviour into thinking about the development of self-regulation and how to encourage behaviour change. Fundamental to this is the complex subject of motivation. How do we ensure that learners *want* to behave in the ways that we need? How do we encourage them to reflect on and improve their own behaviour, inside and outside the classroom environment? How can we make focusing on learning seem like the best of all possible options? During my career, I have moved around phases, teaching in primary and secondary schools, teaching and leading an Early Years setting, and educating teachers and other adults as well. I have had the chance to think about the ways in which our education system does and does not join up, especially when it comes to behaviour. One noticeable aspect of this is how, in Early Years, children are encouraged to be independent, make choices based on personal agency and build on their interests. But as they go through the system, the pressures (and some particularly problematic accountability measures around inspection and test/exam results) mitigate against this. A question to consider is: 'What are the barriers to this agency continuing as young people grow up?'

In recent years, the climate around behaviour has become increasingly divided, with some schools using what are described as 'no excuses' or 'zero tolerance' systems and others choosing what are known as 'restorative' or 'trauma-informed' approaches. These 'no excuses' systems are based around an ultra-consistent approach, in which flexibility and adjustments are minimised. Specific behaviours are demanded from the learners, such as 'tracking' the teacher with their eyes. The 'restorative' approaches focus on dialogue and talking through the issues that occur, with the aim of restoring relationships and attempting to create behaviour change. However, when I talk with colleagues about their views on behaviour, I do not encounter the divisive and binary approaches that we see on social media. Rather, most teachers recognise the complex realities of real-life classrooms, contexts and children, and this makes for a far more nuanced conversation.

Teachers must get on with handling the behaviour of the actual learners who are in their classrooms, regardless of what their school systems might be. Having talked with thousands of teachers about this topic, even though their philosophies might vary, the realities are obvious to all. Yes, it could be argued that detentions 'work' in secondary schools to manage learners, but equally it can be argued that they do little to ultimately change behaviour in the long term. I hope to encourage my readers to think about behaviour in the same way that we think about other types of learning. If a child is struggling to learn to read, we put scaffolds, strategies and various other measures in place, to help them to build the necessary skills. So too with behaviour – we can scaffold, support, encourage, motivate and be creative and reflective in our attempts to support behaviour change. If our focus is on *learning* rather than on *behaving*, what do we want young people to learn while they are in our care?

Above all, this book is designed to be a realistic, honest and useful guide to the kinds of approaches that support children to learn key self-regulation skills. If we come at the question of 'behaviour' from the angle of learning and development, rather than the angle of management and control, we can help all our children and young people to change, develop and grow.

Sue Cowley
www.suecowley.co.uk

Please note that I use the terms 'learners' and 'children and young people' in this book, to be inclusive of all the different contexts in which readers might be working.

Part One

An Introduction to Self-Regulation

Chapter 1
The Importance of Self-Regulation and Metacognition

In this chapter, we will:

- ✓ Explore some of the key terminology in this subject, building a useful working definition.
- ✓ Examine the relationship between self-regulation, self-regulated learning and metacognition.
- ✓ Understand why self-regulation and metacognition are so helpful for long-term outcomes.
- ✓ Explore some of the research into different linked theories within this area of psychology.
- ✓ Understand how these skills enable better relationships between children, peers and adults.
- ✓ Discover what these approaches can offer teachers and learners on a practical level.
- ✓ Explore some key practical strategies for thinking about self-regulation in the classroom.

In recent years, there has been a rapidly increasing level of interest in self-regulation, self-regulated approaches to learning and the metacognitive approaches associated with these areas of learning and development. There is plenty of research to show that these self-regulatory skills are strongly associated with positive outcomes for learners, not just in their formal education but in their adult lives as well. At present, teachers are finding that, in the wake of the pandemic, children and young people are arriving at schools and other educational settings with increased levels of need. These needs seem to cluster particularly around their emotions, their behaviours and their mental health, as well as being linked to levels of resilience and social communication skills. What educators want to know when I work with them is how they can help their learners to develop these skills within the context of the education system that we have at present, with all its complexity and challenge.

Any approach that can help teachers to build young people's coping skills, that encourages them to take active ownership of their behavioural choices and that supports them in learning how to focus, learn and behave is bound to be of benefit. Although it is tempting to lean heavily on systems and policies to manage children and young people's behaviour, what we in fact want them to learn is *how to behave when we are not around to control their behaviours*. By supporting our learners to learn the myriad of skills that go together to form the complex concept of self-regulation, we can offer them benefits that extend way beyond the classroom walls and into wider society beyond.

Before we look in more detail at how we can teach these self-regulation and behavioural skills, it is useful to consider the subject more generally. In the three chapters that form this first part of the book, we look at definitions around self-regulation, why these skills are so important and how this set of skills develops from early childhood. We also explore how and why it is useful to think about behaviour in terms of communication, in order to reframe, rethink and develop our approach to supporting positive behaviours.

Defining terms

The first issue in exploring the subject of self-regulation is defining terms. Depending on which phase of education or stage of childhood researchers are talking about, the terms 'self-regulation', 'metacognition', 'executive function' and 'self-regulated learning' are sometimes used pretty much interchangeably. In addition, the term 'self-regulation' itself encompasses a range of different behaviours, some of which directly impact learning, others of which are more about relationships and social communication between children and their peers, and learners and their teachers, in a classroom or school-based context.

The Education Endowment Foundation, an educational research charity based in England, describes metacognition and self-regulation as having a 'very high impact for very low cost based on extensive evidence' (EEF, 2021). However, in an evidence review for the EEF (Muijs and Bokhove, 2020), it is noted that different researchers define these terms in different ways. Indeed, in several of the EEF summaries, 'self-regulation' refers to aspects of self-regulated learning, rather than the way in which the term is perhaps more commonly understood, particularly in early childhood, i.e. to mean a set of executive functions that support our behaviour, emotions and other aspects such as attentional control.

This complexity is highlighted by the fact that a different reference to self-regulation on the EEF website describes it as 'moderate impact for very low cost based on very limited evidence' (EEF, 2023). This alternative reference is about children's gradually developing abilities to manage their own behaviours and various aspects of their learning, i.e. the way that self-regulation is defined in the Early Years curriculum and a key topic in this book. In this part of the EEF website, helping children to talk and think about their behaviours is identified as being likely to help both in Early Years settings and in their learning at school. Ideally, we need to join up the work being done in different phases around self-regulation, self-regulated learning and metacognitive approaches because it is all part of the same topic.

The variety of definitions of the term 'self-regulation' perhaps helps to underline the wide range of skills that fall under this umbrella term and the various ways in which these skills overlap and interweave. This is dependent on age and stage, with the key skills developing over time as children and young people grow older, at least partly due to their gradually developing brains. For instance, a common issue that teachers highlight with 'behaviour' in secondary classrooms is when learners struggle to focus and direct their attention. However, this same 'behaviour issue' might instead be seen as a developmental and pedagogical aspect of learning in an Early Years setting, where we would not yet necessarily expect children to be developmentally ready to pay extended focus and attention. In writing this book, I have come to understand just how entwined many of these skills are and, in turn, how similar strategies and approaches can work to support the development of different aspects of self-regulation. To give one example, developing our ability to 'self-distance' (see Chapter 5, pages 69–70) helps us not only with impulse control but also with attentional control, empathy and emotional regulation.

The impulse or inhibitory control skills that are so crucial for success in both learning and wider society are not yet fully developed in children in the Early Years. These skills, linked to the development of the prefrontal cortex, only fully come into play from around the age of five years onwards. In other words, we need to be realistic about what we expect from children at different developmental stages. Where children have special educational needs, some of the skills and understanding that are required for aspects such as social communication and empathy are much later developing (if at all). I am often struck, when looking at the various demands of the curriculum on our youngest learners around self-regulatory skills, by how many adults fail to rise to some of these complex psychological and emotional expectations.

Self-regulated learning

The term 'self-regulated learning' has been described by educational researcher Ernesto Panadero as 'an extraordinary umbrella' (Panadero, 2017), which includes many variables related to learning, with a range of different models available to explore. Within the various self-regulated learning models described in this paper, we see many of the terms typically used in relation to concepts of self-regulation, such as 'emotion', 'coping', 'goal setting', 'co-regulation' and so on. Perhaps the uniting factor between concepts of 'self-regulated learning' and 'self-regulation' is that one generally describes approaches to academic tasks while the other deals more with social communication, classroom behaviours and regulating of social interactions. There is clearly a complex mix of the two going on in a typical lesson or normal school day, requiring learners to develop a wide set of complementary skills to attain the best outcomes in their learning.

The EEF evidence review poses the question 'What is self-regulated learning?' (Muijs and Bokhove, 2020, p. 5). In answering the question, the term 'self-regulation' is used, which is described as learners who are 'aware of their strengths and weaknesses' and 'the strategies they use to learn', as well as learners that 'can motivate themselves to engage in learning, and can develop strategies and tactics to enhance learning' (p. 5). If we consider the skills involved in areas such as emotional self-regulation, empathy, facing challenges, coping with failure and paying attention to the right things, and we see them as *part of* learning rather than as separate from it, then we can see the overlap between academic self-regulated learning and learning to 'behave' in a more general sense. Learning itself is a complex experience involving the interplay of a range of cognitive, social, physical, psychological and emotional factors. The definition currently preferred by the Department for Education (DfE) and Ofsted, where learning is defined as being indicated by a 'change in long-term memory' (Ofsted, 2019, p. 19), underplays the complex experience of being a learner.

The development of self-regulation

The EEF evidence review (Muijs and Bokhove, 2020) discusses the interesting question of when these skills develop. For instance, until relatively recently, many researchers thought that metacognition was a relatively late-developing capability, but this position has become increasingly untenable as more research has been conducted in this field and with younger children. David Whitebread, an expert on self-regulation in the early years, argues that metacognitive skills develop early – perhaps as early as three or four years old. Whitebread suggests that young children's skills in this area are obscured by their lack of verbal ability to respond to hypothetical questions from researchers (Whitebread and Basilio, 2012). Similarly, we can see in some of the research currently being conducted into empathy that, in fact, these skills develop much earlier than might previously have been thought. For instance, at around 18 months old, babies can demonstrate altruistic traits towards other people, offering a researcher the food that they appear to prefer over another food that they appear to find disgusting (Barragan et al., 2020).

Language and self-regulation are closely linked because the development of verbal skills allows children to start to verbalise the things that they already 'understand'. In turn, they can use language to start to plan their behaviours and approaches and to 'think through' their learning. Young children's interactions with others (what are often referred to as 'serve and return' interactions) are key for healthy brain development, and they also allow children to experience and respond to other people's reactions to their behaviours. This, in turn, is part of the concept of 'co-regulation', where children develop self-regulation by working to manage their behaviours alongside a caregiver. Although self-regulation skills start to develop in early childhood, a time at which brain development is at its fastest, they also continue to develop through adolescence and into early adulthood.

The Center on the Developing Child at Harvard University published a very useful paper describing the development of these executive functions (2011), and noted that many of these skills can already be seen by the age of three. By this stage, many children can organise themselves to complete a task that involves two rules – for instance, sorting items into piles of two different colours. While these foundational capabilities are in place early on – directing attention, bearing rules in mind, controlling impulses and carrying out plans – they are gradually refined and developed with age. As the tasks that children and young people are asked to do become increasingly complicated and they are asked to follow additional levels of instruction, these skills gradually become honed. Scientists are finding out more and more about the areas of the brain linked to these developing skills, with the prefrontal cortex, the anterior cingulate, the parietal cortex and the hippocampus all being involved. The gradual acquisition of the skills involved corresponds to the way in which these brain regions develop from early childhood through to adolescence.

Theory of mind

As part of the complex picture when trying to find a working definition for this subject, the concept known as 'theory of mind' acts as a key precursor of metacognition, but also links to the development of empathy. Simply put, theory of mind is the idea that we can 'place ourselves' in the minds of others, to understand what their beliefs might be and to see that sometimes their beliefs can be incorrect or startlingly different to our own. A useful practical example of this is seen in a narrative used in research where a child eats half a chocolate bar and puts the remainder in the kitchen cupboard, before going to play outside (Frith and Frith, 2005). While he is outside, his mother finds the chocolate bar and puts it in the fridge. The researchers pose the question: 'Where will Maxi look for his chocolate bar when he returns to the kitchen?'

The very youngest children, who have not yet developed a theory of mind, will think that he looks in the fridge, assuming that what they know to be correct will be what everyone else thinks. However, by around the age of four or five, children will understand that Maxi has what is called a 'false belief' and that he will think it is still in the cupboard. Even much younger children will look at the cupboard first and be surprised if Maxi looks in the fridge. This ability to place ourselves in the mind of someone else is harder for children who have autism and, for some, only develops much later. In turn, this skill links to the concept of empathy, where we 'place ourselves' in the minds of others, to try to see things as others experience them. We mentally put ourselves into their shoes.

The concept of 'theory of mind' helpfully demonstrates the close links between metacognition, self-regulated learning and self-regulation. By learning that others think about their world from their own perspectives, we start to appreciate the flexibility of our minds and our behaviours, and the power of what goes on inside our brains. Finding a definition of self-regulation inevitably requires us to refer to the executive functions that are involved in all three of these areas of learning and development. By learning how to put ourselves 'inside' the mind of someone else, we learn that it is possible to change our beliefs, adapt our thinking and consequently manage and improve both our learning and our behaviours.

The 'marshmallow experiment'

Perhaps the most famous experiment into aspects of self-regulation, particularly around what is called 'inhibitory control', is the study that has become known as the 'marshmallow experiment'. This famous experiment was conducted by psychologist Walter Mischel at Stanford University in the 1970s (Mischel and Ebbesen, 1970). It tested children's ability to 'delay gratification' – in other words, to put up with short-term difficulty or discomfort for the promise of a greater reward in the longer term. As any teacher will appreciate, this ability is fundamental to success in the classroom. Sometimes we will find learning hard, but we must slog on to achieve the desired outcome. Sometimes we will not be in the mood to cooperate or work, but if we can motivate ourselves to focus, our outcomes will be better in the longer term.

In the experiment, children were offered one marshmallow (or pretzel) immediately, but if they were able to wait about 15 minutes, they would be given a second treat. You can see videos of children undertaking this exercise on the internet, and it is very interesting to note how closely their reactions and behaviours mirror those that we see from the learners in our classrooms. Some children will sit on their hands; others will look away or move away from temptation; some will prod the sweet; others will eat the marshmallow immediately. The children have learned that, to resist giving in to their impulses, they need to distract themselves from the immediate temptation (referred to as 'self-distancing', a technique that is explored in more detail in Chapter 5).

In follow-up studies, taking place over many years, researchers found that when children could wait –when they could resist temptation to give in to the immediate urge to eat the marshmallow – their longer-term outcomes were much more positive (Mischel, 2014). These children settled better into school, did better in tests, had higher levels of educational attainment and had other more positive outcomes in their lives generally, such as with their health. Various follow-up studies identified the nuances in the findings – for instance, the effect of whether the children felt that they could put trust in what they were being promised. There were also various cultural differences between how well children would comply with the researcher's request. In addition, the findings seemed to correlate closely with specific home backgrounds. The balance in how self-regulation develops, through nurture or as part of genetics and the environment more generally, is still in question. However, the skill of delayed (or deferred) gratification is clearly an important one for children, particularly in the context of what we ask of them in a school environment.

Self-determination theory

Self-determination theory (CSDT, 2024) is a framework for the study of human motivation and personality, and as such it sits within the various concepts that are linked with self-regulation. The theory looks at how we can support learners to feel motivated to grow, develop and face challenges – all parts of self-regulation and self-regulated learning. It is concerned with intrinsic motivation – the desire to behave appropriately 'for its own sake' – and how we can support wellbeing through meeting people's psychological needs. The goal behind this theory is essentially to find ways in which to educate children to become self-directed and lifelong learners. This is very similar to the way in which supporting them to develop self-regulation will help them to become better able to manage their lives, to learn and to grow both inside and outside the school environment.

Key tenets within self-determination theory include autonomy, competence and relatedness. These are seen as basic psychological needs that are important to meet in order to promote learning, motivation and wellbeing. The idea is that we need to have agency, to feel a sense of success and to feel connected to other human beings in order to operate at our best and become intrinsically motivated. Mindfulness is seen as a foundation for the autonomous regulation of behaviour, which again echoes both metacognition (i.e. thinking about our own thinking) and skills related to our sensory responses, such as interoception (see Chapters 2 and 7), which are closely linked to emotional self-regulation.

People have a natural tendency to internalise the values and behavioural regulations in the world around them and to make these values their own. Self-determination theory suggests that there is a continuum to how our behaviours are controlled by either external or internal demands, described as external, introjected, identified and integrated regulation:

- External regulation is about behaviours being controlled by external demands and pressures, which in a classroom context might mean the threat of sanctions or the promise of rewards.
- Introjected regulation is about what a person feels internally – whether they do an activity because they feel that it will help them to obtain something positive or avoid something negative – again, in a classroom context, this relates to the use of extrinsic motivators.
- Identified regulation is about those behaviours where the individual recognises and identifies with the values of the activity – they want to 'do the right thing'.
- Integrated regulation demonstrates the highest level of internalisation, where the activities become an expression of yourself – in other words, what is referred to as 'self-actualisation' in models such as Maslow's hierarchy of needs.

Interestingly, when thinking about self-determination, at present we are seeing teachers concerned that they do not have as much autonomy or agency as they would like within the system. This might be in terms of the kind of curriculum that they are able to offer their learners, the emphasis that they are asked to put on academic success, perhaps even over mental health and wellbeing, or in the way that accountability often feels like it is 'done to' rather than 'done with' the profession. This, in turn, leads to difficulties around the motivation and retention of teachers – clearly, autonomy and agency are vital for motivation and self-regulation at different ages, including for us as adults.

The role of extrinsic and intrinsic motivators

Thinking about self-regulation, and particularly in relation to what goes on in classrooms, an interesting and complex question to explore is around the impact of the use of extrinsic rewards on the development of self-regulation skills. In other words, what effect do extrinsic rewards (i.e. rewards external to the person) have on internal and more intrinsic motivations to behave and learn? Research (Le Courtois, n.d.) demonstrates that intrinsic motivation is a positive feature of learning – it can lead to more creativity and better analytical performance. In addition, where learners are intrinsically motivated, they tend to choose more challenging tasks. On the other hand, where tasks are 'mindless', extrinsic rewards can be beneficial to motivation. However, a common, consistent finding within the evidence base is that rewards used in a controlling way are likely to undermine intrinsic motivation.

When we say to our learners, 'If you do X, then you get Y', this seems to change their view of the importance of learning that particular thing. They start to do it to get the reward, rather than doing it because it feels like the 'right thing to do'. This, in turn, can lead to the learners becoming passive and preferring easier tasks that might get them an extrinsic reward. Interestingly, not all extrinsic rewards work in the same way. It is the contingent rewards ('If you do X, you get Y') that are particularly problematic for intrinsic motivation. Various studies seem to show that rewards that are not linked to performance do not have this same damaging effect, and that different kinds of reward will work differently as well. Extrinsic classroom rewards that are symbolic, such as certificates, do not seem to have quite such a problematic effect as those that are based on the value of what is being offered.

Some researchers suggest that, because school is not always naturally intrinsically motivating to our learners, extrinsic rewards are necessary. However, while children generally start their educational careers with a keen interest in learning, this has been shown to drop as they go through the system. Is it that they are effectively being 'trained' by our use of extrinsic rewards, or is it that learning just gets harder and has less potential to be intrinsically motivating? In this context, it is interesting to explore what happens in different educational contexts – for instance, the motivation that many home-educated learners seem to show when allowed to direct their own learning. In the Early Years setting that I have helped to run for over 15 years, we made the decision not to use any extrinsic rewards about a decade ago, and we have not used any since. Our view was that our young children are sufficiently well motivated by an intrinsic desire to play and learn, and we did not want to interfere with this to the detriment of their intrinsic motivation.

The importance of self-regulation

As we can see by exploring aspects of, theories about and potential definitions of self-regulation, it is a skill that allows children and young people to better manage themselves as learners and to better handle being within a school context, in which social communication plays such an important role. Self-regulation enables learners to manage their thoughts, ideas, approaches, emotions, perspectives, behaviours and attention, and to face and overcome challenges in their learning. If teachers were to describe what they see as an 'ideal learner', this description would probably cover many of the bases. These are certainly skills that we have the potential to help our learners to build and develop.

As adults, we need to be able to multitask, to manage our impulses and to follow multiple-step directions even when we are interrupted or when there are distractions. We need to be able to remain focused on what we are doing and take deliberate, intentional steps towards the goals that we want to achieve in our daily lives. Put together, these skills allow us to solve tricky problems and make sensible decisions; they enable us to persist when an important task is difficult to complete; and they allow us to recognise our mistakes and take steps to solve or overcome them. Working together, these skills will help our learners to face the myriad challenges that exist in the modern world and, in turn, become empathetic, helpful and valued members of wider society. In addition, as has already been noted, these skills are closely linked to positive outcomes in terms of educational success and a sense of wellbeing more widely in our lives.

A working definition of self-regulation

Having explored some of the theories, concepts and definitions that fall under the umbrella term of 'self-regulation', 'metacognition' and 'self-regulated learning', it felt useful for me to come up with a working definition of the term that links to the focus and approach within this book. It is tricky to find a definition that encompasses the wide set of skills that we will be exploring here, but the definition below summarises the key points that will be examined.

> Self-regulation is our gradually developing ability to understand and manage our thoughts, feelings, impulses, attitudes and behaviours and those of others. It is a skill that promotes learning, supports wellbeing and aids effective social communication.

Practical strategies for the classroom

As well as understanding why self-regulation is important, it is also useful to help your learners understand the importance and value of self-regulation approaches and how these influence their behaviours and emotions. By talking with learners about this, we can boost their understanding of how learning works. Consider where in the curriculum you can make space to do this important work, encouraging your learners to think metacognitively about how their brains work to support better behaviour.

- ✓ Talk with your learners about how their brains develop and work and why it is so important and helpful for them to focus on doing this. With younger learners, this might simply be about references to how 'talk helps build our brains' or 'we can learn how to regulate our emotions', while with older learners you could delve deeper into the science of how learning happens in the brain. Try not to see this as information known only by teachers, to help us find classroom strategies, but rather as a fascinating part of the overall dynamics of how learning works.
- ✓ Introduce young people to concepts around different self-regulation skills – for instance, the idea that failure is part and parcel of the way in which we learn, encouraging them to see it as a positive. Many educators use the acronym 'FAIL' as a 'first attempt in learning', as a way to get this concept over to their learners.
- ✓ Talk to your learners about how 'mistakes grow our brains' and how we can 'fail forwards', i.e. learn from our errors, by thinking about what we could do differently next time around. Consider how these concepts might be best explained, depending on the context and age of your class.
- ✓ Model a positive attitude to your own self-regulation skills, talking about how sometimes you fail to manage your emotions or struggle to control your impulses. If you get wound up or snappy with the class, see this as an opportunity to talk things through and show your learners that it is possible to apologise and not feel like you are losing face or status.
- ✓ Do not be afraid to be explicit about this – as a teacher, you are modelling an attitude to learning from which your learners are constantly learning. This applies as much to things like emotional regulation as it does to subject-based content and understanding.

Practical approaches to motivation

The field of motivation is a complex area within the topic of self-regulation, with various potential issues around the use of extrinsic motivators, particularly for vulnerable learner groups such as looked-after children. From a practical perspective, it is useful to highlight some key considerations and best practice approaches, because most schools in the UK still use extrinsic motivators as part of their behaviour policy. For those readers interested in thinking about how they might adapt and develop their thinking around this topic, the following suggestions should support that process.

When thinking about the use of extrinsic motivators, remember:

- ✓ They can elicit feelings of shame, especially if given in public – for instance, in those learners who have missed out.
- ✓ This is particularly so when thinking about rewards given to whole groups, where an individual might 'stop' the group from receiving the reward, for example in 100 per cent attendance rewards for a class.
- ✓ Some uses of extrinsic motivators can encourage a fixed rather than a growth mindset, with learners developing a 'what's in it for me?' mentality.
- ✓ On a more positive note, extrinsic motivators can act as a marker or symbol of progress.
- ✓ This means that they can be particularly useful for some learners who have special needs and who benefit from additional reassurance.

To make the most of extrinsic motivators, keep the following ideas in mind:

- ✓ The best motivators of all are those that reflect staff/learner relationships – that give learners the message that you 'believe in them'.
- ✓ The most powerful rewards are often about time, attention and kindness, rather than a 'thing'.
- ✓ Often, the best motivators are creative – ones that are funny, ironic, amusing, surprising or unusual.
- ✓ A reward received unexpectedly is much more powerful in promoting motivation than one that a learner gets contingent on something that they did.
- ✓ Rewards that are earned through cooperation can be powerful in promoting positive peer group relationships. However, see the note above about not making individuals feel that a group 'missed out' on an anticipated reward because of them.
- ✓ Having what they have done seen and noted by other adults can be a strong motivator for children and young people.
- ✓ At the same time, some learners really benefit from positive praise and rewards being given privately and quietly, perhaps because they feel that they have a 'reputation' to maintain.
- ✓ Remember that rewards are not just about academic attainment – in the context of supporting the development of self-regulation skills, focus on social and emotional attainment as well.

Chapter 2
Self-Regulation: What It Is and How It Develops

In this chapter, we will:

✓ Get an overview of some of the brain processes involved in self-regulation.
✓ Explore the different skills that fall under the umbrella term of self-regulation.
✓ Identify and examine different aspects of self-regulatory control.
✓ Consider the impact of the home environment on how self-regulation develops.
✓ Examine the kind of issues that can cause difficulties with the development of self-regulation.
✓ Explore some key practical strategies for building partnerships with parents and carers.

As we saw in the previous chapter, self-regulation encompasses a wide and complex set of interrelated skills. These skills develop over the course of childhood, into adolescence and early adulthood, and this chapter provides an overview of them. While they are with us, our learners are not only learning academic subjects, but they are also learning 'how to behave'. For the purposes of this book, the term 'self-regulation' is used to describe the set of executive functions that are linked to being aware of, understanding and managing our own behaviours. However, the aim here is to see 'behaviour' as being meant in the widest possible sense, including all those behaviours that contribute to learning and to emotional and social wellbeing in a classroom environment.

When we think and talk about school classrooms, understandably we tend to think of 'managing behaviours' from the teacher's perspective – how do we manage these children or young people in order to enable learning to take place? How do we stop them from 'misbehaving' so that we can get on with teaching? And yet so many of the teachers I meet describe 'low-level misbehaviours' to me that are essentially symptoms of poor skill development in the field of self-regulation. If a learner is off-task, this may indicate that they are struggling to focus; if a learner does not follow instructions, it could well be that they struggled to pay full attention while the teacher was explaining a task. Similarly, if a child or young person goes into a full 'meltdown' and loses all emotional control, clearly there is a set of skills in emotional regulation that they are missing. By thinking about learning in the round, rather than by simply using the 'learning = memory' definition currently favoured by education policymakers, we can start to clearly see the complex interplay of behaviour and subject-based learning.

This chapter explores the self-regulatory processes that allow individuals to learn how to 'manage' their behaviours for themselves, whether this is about impulse control (being able to wait), emotional regulation (staying calm, coping well with difficulties), attentional control (directing our focus to the 'right thing' in terms of what we need to do to learn), empathy (being able to position ourselves 'in the place of' another to see a different perspective) and so on. The approaches that support the development of these skills can be used alongside a typical school behaviour policy, as part of supporting learners to regulate and control their behaviours. It may be worth considering some of the findings explored in the book to challenge yourself about the contents of your behaviour policy, particularly if you are in a leadership role – for instance, understanding more about the potential impact of repeated sanctions on a young person's self-concept and considering how it might be possible to support a more positive self-image in your learners.

Self-regulation and executive function

Self-regulation skills are the mental processes or executive functions that allow us to do things like planning, juggling tasks, handling difficult emotions and directing our attention to the right things. The brain processes involved in self-regulation include working memory, mental flexibility and self (or impulse) control. These three aspects of our brains come together to allow us to usefully manage our daily lives. A very useful metaphor for this, shared on the brilliantly informative Harvard Center on the Developing Child website (n.d.), is to think of these skills like an air traffic control system. Effectively, these are the skills that stop us from 'bumping into' other people and help us to avoid getting into difficult situations, socially, physically or cognitively.

1. *Working memory*

    The first of the skills required for self-regulation is our working memory. The best way to understand working memory is to think of it as the ability to retain a small amount of information and manipulate it in our minds – a kind of cognitive 'sketch pad' if you like. The reason why working memory is so closely linked to self-regulation is because we need to 'think things through' to regulate our behaviours. For instance, if our teacher gives us a series of instructions, we need to be able to hold these in our minds as we complete them one after another. Our working memory helps us to pay attention, retain the information in the very short term, and work towards completing the series of tasks that we have been asked to do.

2. *Mental flexibility*

   The second of the skills required for self-regulation is mental flexibility, which is about the ability to come at challenges and problems from different angles. As human beings, we are naturally inclined to think in a linear way – we tend to come at problems from the same angle, over and over again, and then we get frustrated when nothing changes or we are not successful. However, when we need to solve problems and come up with solutions to challenges, it is typically the case that it is better to think sideways and to use what is referred to as 'lateral thinking' to come up with a solution. Mental flexibility is about trying the novel or the unusual route, and being willing to take risks in our thinking and our approaches. A key aspect of self-regulation linked to this skill is around goal-setting behaviours and coping with challenges and failure. When we set ourselves a goal that we do not reach, we need to have the adaptability and flexibility to know that we can change tack or try a new approach, to cope with the difficult feeling that we might have failed.

3. *Impulse control*

   The third aspect of self-regulation – our impulse control – allows us to 'pause' our instinctive reactions to situations and experiences. Inhibitory control helps us to take a reasoned and rational approach, which, in turn, is more likely to lead to more successful outcomes. Impulse control develops with age, due to the maturation of the brain (although you can probably think of some adults who still struggle with this aspect of self-regulation). Impulse control is closely linked to deferred gratification because it allows us to work towards a hard, longer-term goal, controlling our impulse to give up or give in when things get tough.

As a set of skills, these are all vital for learning and development and for the kinds of 'behaviours' that as educators we would like to see in our schools and settings. Although we are not born with these skills, they are skills that we can be supported to develop. Adults can work alongside children to scaffold the development of these skills, in a process known as 'co-regulation'. Eventually, the aim is for children and young people to be able to do these things independently of adults and independently of the systems that we create to manage our classrooms. A useful way in which to think about this is to ask: 'What do I want the learners to do when I am not in the room, as well as when I am?'

What is self-regulation?

A useful way to understand all the different areas of development that self-regulation includes is to describe it using a series of simple diagrams. Many of the areas that come under this umbrella term are interlinked and interdependent. For instance, emotional regulation ties in with the development of empathy; the ability to set and achieve learning goals links with being able to cope with challenges and failure. You can find a brief description of each area of self-regulation below. The chapters that follow dig more deeply into each area in turn and suggest practical strategies that you can use in your classroom to help develop each aspect of self-regulation.

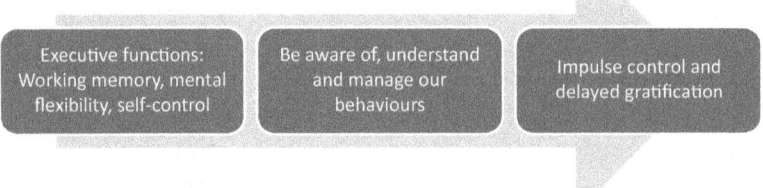

The process of self-regulation starts with the executive functions of working memory, mental flexibility and inhibitory control. As described in the figure above, these work together as a kind of 'air traffic control system' for our lives, both personally and within wider society. The skills that these executive functions enable us to master are crucial for learning and for social communication.

Managing our behaviours

First and foremost, we need to become conscious and aware of our own 'behaviours' – that what we are doing is called 'behaving'. In the youngest children, you will often see that they are almost completely unaware that they are getting themselves wound up, that they are lashing out at others or that they are behaving in a way that others might interpret as 'difficult' or 'defiant'. The behaviour almost seems to 'take over' their entire self. Gradually, as we age, we start to become more competent with our behavioural skills. Once we become conscious or aware that we are 'behaving' (for instance, acting in an angry and confrontational way to others by lashing out or shouting at them), we then need to try to understand what is motivating our behaviour or where it comes from (for example, having low blood sugar levels or being upset because we feel unfairly treated).

The final part of the process of being able to 'manage' our own behaviours is to learn how to control and calm ourselves down – for example, by getting something to eat or going for a walk to improve our mood, or by counting down from ten or trying some breathing exercises. Obviously in a classroom situation it is complicated by the fact that we have 30 or so learners, all 'behaving' simultaneously. It is not possible for them to just take a break to calm down because schools do not work like that. However, it might be a reasonable adjustment to say that one learner who experiences sensory overload could take themselves out of the room for a 'brain break' when they need one. The more that we can encourage all our learners to take responsibility for their *own* behaviour and to come up with their *own* solutions, the better things will be for us as teachers.

Where we face what we might call 'poor behaviours' in a classroom context, it is tempting to think that these are intentional, and indeed, sometimes, that may well be the case. However, it is a much more complex picture than at first it might appear. It is perfectly possible for poor behaviours to arise from personal or environmental factors that are nothing to do with a learner 'deciding' to behave inappropriately. For instance, a young person with sensory processing difficulties who has a meltdown due to sensory overload may need an adult's co-regulatory support to help them return to a regulated state. Some educators claim that 'the system' should do all the work, and all that is needed is clear and consistent punitive consequences for inappropriate behaviour. They say that the teacher's role is to teach, not to 'manage behaviour'. Unfortunately, this overlooks the fact that behaviour itself is part of the curriculum in some phases and areas, as well as the role of emotions and behaviours in a classroom context, especially when we are talking about younger learners or learners from troubled backgrounds. We need a certain level of awareness and the ability to look at ourselves and our behaviours rationally if we are going to understand and manage them. Where poor behaviour escalates in the classroom environment, this is often because the learner's emotional 'fight or flight' response (sometimes also called the 'fight, flight or flock' response) has kicked in and they no longer have their impulses under their rational control.

Impulse control and delayed gratification

Our impulse control allows us to inhibit our instant, impulsive reactions to the situations in which we find ourselves. In a difficult situation, we might feel the impulse to lash out, swear or shout, but we can develop the ability to inhibit this response. In a situation where we feel tempted to do something that we really should not do, it is our impulse control that allows us to say 'no'. It is important to understand that impulse control develops over time and that children only gradually become more able to inhibit their reactions. Impulsive behaviours are normal and to be expected in young children – their impulsivity helps them to learn because they are curious, they move around a lot and chatter about what they are doing excitedly. These are all features of a busy, active Early Years learner. Gradually, they learn to sublimate some of these behaviours, to fit into the wider social context (and also to make a classroom situation workable). For instance, learning to wait your turn when playing a game, rather than to snatch or grab, is important in being able to make friends.

The ability to delay or defer gratification helps us to slog through the more challenging and difficult experiences that we have – knowing that even though something is difficult in the short term, it will be beneficial in the longer term. School requires a great deal of impulse control and delayed gratification – we cannot always be the one being picked as a volunteer by the teacher; we cannot spend all our time doing only those subjects that we find easy, interesting or enjoyable. Impulse control allows us to build key skills for the classroom, such as taking turns, sharing, listening and paying careful attention. These are the skills that children and young people need to master in order to avoid the 'low-level misbehaviour' that is so problematic for teachers. It is not surprising to see self-regulation appear as a key skill in the curriculum – for instance, as an early learning goal in the EYFS in England.

| Maintain focus, direct attention, manage distractions | Be aware of strong feelings, find self-calming strategies | Empathise – see other perspectives |

Attentional control

Looking at this next diagram, self-regulation allows us to keep our focus on the right thing – again, essential for success in education. In the classroom, we need to be able to direct our attention to the right thing (what our teacher/peer is saying/what is on the interactive whiteboard) and manage any distractions that might interrupt our learning (our peers/the weather conditions outside/a wasp in the room). We also need to learn to concentrate and focus on learning for extended periods of time as we move through the education system, eventually building up to far more extended periods of concentration in our final exams. The world is a busy, noisy, highly sensory place, and so we must train our brains to filter out the sensory information that is not helpful, to allow us to focus on what we do want or need to think about. Classrooms are typically full of potential distractions – being drawn off-task by the chatter of peers, having our attention wander to look out of the window at an unexpected noise outside, a wasp buzzing around the room on a summer's day. All teachers understand just how easily learners can be distracted from the content of a lesson.

Like so many other aspects of self-regulation, the impulse that we are trying to control here is one that is important in terms of our evolution. A baby's impulse to cry when they are hungry ensures that they get fed – the behaviour that we eventually learn to control or sublimate is essentially what keeps us alive when we are tiny. Similarly, the impulsive behaviours of toddlers help them to explore and interact with their world, taking risks and experimenting, which is all part and parcel of learning.

Emotional regulation and empathy

Our gradually developing awareness of our own feelings and emotions is an important stage in children's development. At first, young children focus on physical sensations, learning about their environment through their sensory interactions with it, gradually developing the ability to coordinate their bodies. At this early stage, they are egocentric, without a developed understanding of their own emotional state or a clearly established sense of how other people have minds and emotions of their own. Gradually, through their interactions with others and through adult scaffolding and supportive co-regulation techniques, children start to understand the feelings that they experience. They begin to learn the names that we put to these emotions, and can be supported to understand what causes them, by focusing on how experiences and situations make their bodies feel.

Interestingly, the term 'feelings' literally describes our ability to experience sensations in our bodies (a knot in our stomach, a nauseous sensation) and to link these to an emotion, such as being anxious or scared. This ability to scrutinise our own internal sensations and to interpret them is called interoception. It is often described as an extra sense, in addition to the five senses that we normally think about. By tuning into our bodies, we attune ourselves to our emotional state. Of course, classrooms are highly social places, full of strong emotions, both positive and negative, with lots of potential for frustration when learning or peer group relationships feel difficult. We need children and young people to understand how to calm themselves and their emotions as part of their developing self-regulation skills, but at the same time without denying that these emotions exist and are valid.

Goal-oriented behaviours, challenge and failure

> Setting and achieving goals → Coping well with challenge and failure → A 'can do' attitude – linked to sense of self

The final set of areas of self-regulation, shown in this diagram, link very clearly to the learning that goes on in the classroom because they are essentially linked to task completion. It is very important that our learners learn to set themselves realistic goals, which they are motivated to work to achieve, as part of the process of becoming self-regulated learners. For learners to achieve their goals, they must become comfortable with both challenge and failure. It is only through trying and failing, and trying again, that the process of learning can take place. When teachers talk about resilience, we are talking about how children and young people cope with challenges, setbacks, difficulties and so on, without giving up, giving in or feeling a sense of emotional dysregulation. An interesting question to ask ourselves is exactly how resilient we believe our learners should be, and how much adults need to help by softening difficulties to help them cope, especially given the multitude of challenges that face them in their world at present.

Interestingly, the system itself can often mitigate against this process of trying and failing. Our learners are constantly sent both conscious and subconscious messages about the importance of 'not failing'. This happens both through the way in which the exam system works and also through the way in which the accountability system encourages us to approach learning. It is hard to push back against the urge to over-help our learners because we are primed to focus on achieving 'good outcomes'. We know that the system may judge us as 'failing' if we do not increase learners' test and exam scores or get them to keep their books neat and tidy. At the same time, though, we must accept that to cope with failure, learners need to be allowed to experience it. A key way in which we can help ourselves to avoid the urge to over-help and over-scaffold is to praise the struggle and the resilience required to approach a task, instead of the outcome achieved (or not achieved). This links in closely to Carol Dweck's work on a 'growth mindset' – the idea that we want to encourage our learners to understand that with effort, application and persistence, they can continue to learn and grow (see Further Reading for details).

Learner agency

Goal setting and striving to meet challenges are essential elements of the sense of self that is required for young people to fully self-regulate. When learners perceive that the choices and decisions that they make will have a genuine impact on their experience of their world, they will be more motivated to keep trying and pushing forwards. Where the goals and challenges that we set our learners are too difficult or, conversely, too easy, this can impact negatively on their motivation. With our support, we can help them through a process of co-regulation to take gradual steps forward in their learning. Ideally, we want to foster a feeling that they can always 'give it a go' and that we will not react negatively if they do not succeed.

This is part of supporting learners to understand that it is OK (and indeed, beneficial) to fail at times – that this is how they push forwards and make improvements. It is important to help learners cope with critique and feedback and to see these as a positive rather than a negative, again separating these features from their sense of self. In other words, just because I struggle to learn something, this does not say anything negative about me as a person. This 'can do' attitude, where learners see the struggle as part of the way in which they improve their own lives, is a central tenet in the development of self-regulation.

How does self-regulation develop?

When a baby is born, their world must feel deeply confused and confusing. They are not yet able to focus and see their surroundings properly, and their senses are not yet operating at their full capacity. They hear a blur of noises, indistinguishable from one another. It is no wonder that a baby homes in on the familiar – the smell of their mother, the sound of their caregivers' voices. Gradually, babies begin to make sense of their world, as their senses develop through their early experiences. This gradually developing understanding is mediated by the interactions that they have with adults. However, babies are still at the stage where they cannot use language to communicate what they need. Although it might be difficult for us when we hear a baby cry, in fact, this is essentially their only way of telling us what they 'need' – crying is an important evolutionary feature, which helps to ensure that babies get their needs met.

We are not born with the skills that allow us to self-regulate but we have the potential to develop them. Although genes play a part in our ability to self-regulate, our early environment and the experiences that we go through in childhood help to shape our brains and build our self-regulation skills. Those early experiences have a very powerful impact on brain development, with around 90 per cent of brain development taking place in the period up to the age of five years old. It is inevitable that we will be working with some learners who have not had the kind of early experiences and interactions that we might want for them, and that they will not have been given the support needed to develop their self-regulation skills.

Adverse experiences during early childhood can have a negative impact on cognitive and physical development, and subsequently on self-regulation skills. For instance, a child who lives in an environment where there is food poverty might struggle to develop the ability to delay gratification. In many ways, this is a natural reaction to a known environmental factor, because they are not secure in the knowledge of where their next meal is coming from. The various factors that influence the early development of self-regulation are summarised in the following two diagrams, with more detailed explanations of the factors involved over the next few pages.

Children need to form secure attachments with carers that they can trust – adults who behave consistently and who build honest, open and trusting relationships with their children. This is important because the child then feels emotionally secure enough to explore, experiment, face challenges and difficulties, and gradually become more independent, through a process of scaffolding and co-regulation. In addition, resources need to be reliably available in order to create that sense of security and certainty. If you do not feel secure and trust that you will be able to get hold of what you need, when you need it (for instance, food), then logically you are more likely to feel the need to get any food that is offered to you.

Thinking about the marshmallow experiment described in Chapter 1 (see pages 12–13), when a child who lives in a home with food poverty is offered a marshmallow, they might grab it or snatch it. They are motivated partly by hunger – what appears to be a lack of impulse control is a survival mechanism. Similarly, if a child has not developed trusting relationships with adults, they might grab the marshmallow for fear that they cannot trust that they will be given another one. In other words, a sense of security is vitally important for the development of self-regulation because it allows us to take calculated risks and to delay our need for gratification.

Children also need to experience plenty of agency to develop self-regulation – to be given the chance to make active choices about what they do and how they do it. This enables them to feel that they can have a direct impact on their experience of their lives, and in turn, feel empowered by the decisions and choices that they make. Interestingly, this means that *overly* structured environments can have a detrimental effect on the development of self-regulation, in addition to the more obvious problems within chaotic environments. The issue with excessive structure is that the child can come to feel like an observer, rather than an active participant in what happens to them. This means that 'helicopter'-type parenting styles, where the carers 'hover over' their child at all times, can be problematic for the development of self-regulation skills. Where parents or carers tend to over-help and over-structure the child's life, the child never learns how to take risks, handle failure or gradually become more responsible.

Children need to face plenty of challenges to help them believe that they can handle difficult situations and cope. The challenges that they need are both physical – for instance, playing outdoors, including in inclement weather – and intellectual – for instance, visiting museums and having access to interesting books. By facing challenges and seeing that they can cope with them, children gradually learn how to manage risk and cope with increasing levels of difficulty. Generally, learners seem to be more able to cope with challenges than we might give them credit for. By raising levels of challenge, at the same time as offering appropriate support, it can be surprising what children and young people can attain.

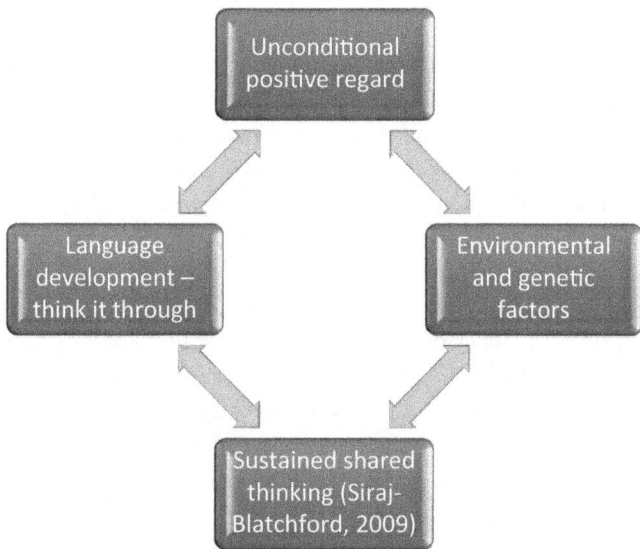

The term 'unconditional positive regard' means helping children to view themselves as separate from, and therefore able to make active decisions about, their behaviours. A useful way of thinking about this is the idea that a carer might say to their child, 'No matter how you behave, I will always love and be there for you.' (Or, in an educational context, 'I will always respect and care for you.') This is not to say that we *ignore* any difficult or challenging behaviour from the children, nor that we *excuse* it and blame the parent or teacher. However, what we need to do is to ensure that the child perceives themselves as *separate from* their behaviour. By helping them to develop this sense of themselves as an individual with agentic control, they gradually come to understand that their behaviour does not define them (even if sometimes they struggle to regulate and their behaviour is poor or unacceptable). Children need to see that they have agency to make changes to the way in which they behave – that they can actively choose to behave differently – and to learn how to control their impulses and make better choices.

There are extensive interconnections between the areas of the brain that support self-regulation and the deeper brain structures that control our responses to threat and stress. For this reason, extended exposure to threatening situations can be detrimental to the development and deployment of the executive function skills described in this book. These kinds of adverse childhood experiences can leave an imprint on our genes, and so environment and genetic makeup of both children and their parents all play a part in the development of self-regulation. The researchers in the 'marshmallow experiment' (Mischel and Ebbesen, 1970) described in the previous chapter identified a link between home background and the ability to defer gratification. Where children have been brought up in a secure, settled, safe, consistent home, they inevitably have access to many of the environmental experiences that support healthy development, and vice versa.

During this early period of child development, the child's carers will (or should) gradually support them to manage more and more aspects of their lives by themselves. Adults create the framework in which this happens, by talking things through, creating routines, offering cues and breaking up tricky tasks into smaller, more achievable chunks – in other words, all the kinds of scaffolding strategies that we see educators deploying in their classrooms to support learning. The term 'sustained shared thinking' describes the kind of interplay of interactions that work together to support children's cognitive development and learning. The carer takes an interest in what the child is doing or saying, asking open-ended questions, making suggestions or offering support and comfort. The child responds by building their learning, asking additional questions or simply sharing their joy. These 'serve and return' interactions are very powerful indeed for learning and brain development.

Many of the various skills encompassed by the term 'self-regulation' depend heavily on language – children need to be able to 'think things through' and narrate their thinking in their minds. This is why self-regulation skills are closely mediated by language development – the more the child has the skills to describe, manipulate and experiment with their thoughts, by thinking things through, the more able they will be to make rational decisions and manage their emotional state. Indeed, as a child's language develops, so does their ability to express themselves and to self-regulate in all the different ways described in this book.

Serve and return

The term 'serve and return' is very similar to the concept of sustained shared thinking. The idea is about a kind of 'dialogue' between a carer and their child, or an educator and a learner. The 'dialogue' can include the use of non-verbal interactions, such as gestures and facial expressions, as well as talking and thinking things through using language. The term 'resonance' is sometimes used to describe effective interactions – the adult and the child work in synchrony, with carers adapting and responding to the child's signals. This kind of mirroring is often seen in classrooms, where you gain the sense of an 'atmosphere' in which the teacher subconsciously matches their patterns of verbal and non-verbal communication with those of the learners, to create a sense of working together to build and sustain the learning.

Although you might often hear people talk about serve and return 'conversations', in fact, it is simply the interactions with carers and others around them that help babies build the architecture of their brains. The term refers to any kind of interaction between a child and a carer – for instance, a parent tickling their baby, the baby laughing in response and the parent responding joyfully to the baby's giggles to encourage them to enjoy and repeat the experience. Where these interactions are warm, responsive and sensitive to the child's needs, this helps to form neural connections and build the architecture of the child's brain. For this reason, in families where the mother has experienced post-natal depression, there can be issues with the sensitive interactions required for brain development. The extent of a parent's ability to interact with their baby using typical facial expressions, gestures and vocal tones can have a direct impact on cognitive development.

The influence of stress

Evidence suggests that stress impacts the underlying neurobiological processes of self-regulation, as well as its cognitive, emotional and behavioural aspects (Murray and Hamoudi, 2016). In other words, it impacts how the brain develops and works. Although a certain amount of stress can increase our focus and help us approach challenges, excessive stress can impair our ability to function. It is useful to think about different kinds of stress – acute and chronic stress – and the different effects that these might have on the development of children's self-regulation skills.

Acute stress involves the body's stress system being activated briefly, in response to a temporary stimulus or situation. Although this can be problematic if the stress is severe enough, our stress response system (or SRS) is usually well-equipped to manage short-term stresses. However, when a person undergoes chronic stress, where the body's SRS is frequently activated or the activation of the SRS happens for long periods of time, this can have negative effects on the brain and on a person's behaviours. When children experience adversity that is strong, frequent and/or prolonged, this can create a toxic stress response. The kind of stressors that might affect children in this way include physical or emotional abuse, neglect, exposure to domestic violence and so on.

Where an individual's life or physical wellbeing is under threat, or where this happens to someone important to them, this can lead to trauma, and the child's ability to cope can be completely overwhelmed. The aftermath of an acute trauma can also become a chronic stressor, with long-lasting consequences – for instance, the impact of sustained homelessness. The body's SRS is over-stimulated, leading to sustained high concentrations of stress hormones. There is plenty of evidence to suggest that this, in turn, has an adverse effect on the development of self-regulation. Bruce Perry's work (n.d.) offers a useful way to understand the effects of the different types of stress. Perry notes that unpredictable stress that is severe and prolonged may lead to vulnerability, whereas predictable stress that is moderate and controlled is more likely to lead to the development of resilience.

Practical strategies for the classroom

Teachers face a tricky situation in that they cannot always know about all the kinds of stresses and traumas that a child or young person might have faced before they first meet them. Although some learners will have been identified as having safeguarding and child protection concerns, the details of these are likely to be confidential. Classroom teachers are unlikely to have a fully rounded picture of the child's prior experiences. In addition, there may be children who have experienced chronic stress and trauma but this has not yet been identified within the education system. Of course, it is also the case that teachers might have a class of 30 or more learners, or numerous large classes with whom they have to work, and this can make responding sensitively to individual circumstances very tricky.

One useful way in which educators can support the development of self-regulation is to share strategies and ideas with parents and carers. No matter how much time you spend in the classroom with your learners, they will always be spending far more time at home with their parents. In education, we often talk about how problematic it is when families do not understand key principles such as setting clear boundaries and acknowledging emotions. However, given that we see such a strong influence of the home on the kinds of behaviour that we see in our settings, it is perhaps surprising that partnerships with parents and carers can sometimes feel under-developed.

Some of the ways in which you might build these partnerships are listed below:

- ✓ Organise workshops to share some of the key principles of the development of self-regulation and, importantly, why these skills are so central to positive outcomes for children – for example, explaining the importance of supporting but not over-helping children.
- ✓ Emphasise these principles in your interactions with parents and carers, whether this is at parent consultation evenings in a secondary school or when they drop off their children in a primary setting. For instance, you might position yourself close to the cloakroom, so that you can model for parents how to encourage their children to hang up their own coats and bags. You could do this by using positive statements such as, 'Hari, why don't you show Dad how responsible and grown-up you are about hanging up your own coat?'
- ✓ Be explicit with parents and carers about what they can do to help their children develop self-regulation skills, giving them specific examples that they can follow – for example, encouraging them to help their child get their bag ready for the next day of school on the evening before.
- ✓ Explain why you need things done in a certain way – for instance, explain why it is important that homework is done without too much adult input, i.e. so that you can accurately assess whether the child has learned something. Do not assume that parents and carers understand education in the same way that you do – their experiences of the system could be at least a couple of decades or more out of date, and may have been negative ones.
- ✓ Avoid nagging parents and carers about all the things that they have not done, as this just gets people's backs up. Aim to stick to a positive message about what they can do to support their children. Where you do have problems with individuals, deal with those on an individual level – in other words, do not blame 100 per cent of parents for the behaviour of one per cent.
- ✓ Whole-school initiatives, such as running a breakfast club, setting up a food bank or creating a pre-used school uniform shop, will obviously be useful for families who are struggling with their financial situation. This, in turn, could help to alleviate some of the potential stress that their children might experience in the home environment.

Chapter 3
Behaviour as Communication: From Co-Regulation to Self-Regulation

In this chapter, we will:

- ✓ Explore the ways in which we use behaviour as a form of communication.
- ✓ Examine how we can reframe behaviour as giving useful feedback.
- ✓ Think about what the term 'co-regulation' means in a classroom context.
- ✓ Examine ways in which to support children to move from co-regulation to self-regulation.
- ✓ Explore how adults can find a balance between over- and under-helping.
- ✓ Consider how to encourage children to become intrinsically motivated to self-regulate.
- ✓ Offer practical strategies to support communication in the classroom.

Although there is some resistance in education to the idea that 'behaviour is communication', particularly on social media, essentially this phrase is just a truism. All behaviours communicate *something* because we are all 'behaving' all the time as human beings, whether we are aware of it or not. In a social context, other people's behaviour can simply be viewed as a form of feedback on our interactions with them – we can choose to act on it or choose not to act on it. When we find ourselves in situations where we are in contact with groups of other human beings, those people will also be interpreting our 'behaviours' to figure out how to interact with us or to interpret what we are doing, thinking or feeling. They might be doing this consciously, but it is just as likely to be a subconscious part of how they intuitively 'read' who and what we are. There is a tendency within education to think of 'behaviour' as meaning a negative, as in the concept of 'poor', 'difficult' or 'challenging' (sometimes described as 'bad' or 'mis') behaviour. However, 'behaviours' can just as easily mean positive ones – smiling and laughing when we are happy or showing that we are interested in and curious about something that happens in a lesson.

One of the key roles that we play in our schools and settings is as the model of a supportive, kind adult who is willing to help learners to build better behaviours. One of the key ways in which we can do this is by looking at how our learners are behaving, interpreting what those behaviours communicate and working alongside the learner to scaffold, support and help them to manage their impulses, emotions and the resulting behaviours. Babies naturally struggle to self-regulate, and it would be completely inappropriate to get cross with them for not being able to do this. A baby's cries are a very important kind of feedback, telling us that they need something from us, whether this is food, comfort, help with pain of some kind and so on. As children get older, they gradually learn to communicate what is going on for them internally, particularly by using language. However, where a child struggles to express what they need, where they find it difficult to manage a situation or where they are unable to interpret the signals that their body is sending them, this can be a useful point for an adult to step in. By co-regulating with our learners, we can help them to explain what they need, scaffold their learning and help them to avoid becoming dysregulated.

Behaviour as feedback

Saying that 'behaviour is communication' is not the same thing as saying that we must pay attention to all behavioural communications in a classroom situation. Clearly, this would not be possible or indeed sensible. Some things that our behaviours communicate are unnecessary, negative and/or best ignored (although exactly when this is the case is very much contextual). For instance, it might be wise to ignore a learner who is communicating that they find a topic 'boring'. However, if we remain open to the possibility that human behaviours give us a useful form of feedback, we might consider some ways in which we could have a go at making that topic more interesting next time around. This might or might not be possible, and you might or might not feel that their critique is justified, but to ignore the feedback completely is to miss an opportunity to improve and develop.

Where we stand on this issue mainly depends on the (typically controversial) question of whether we see behaviour as solely belonging to the learners or whether we believe that there might sometimes be things that teachers can do to encourage positive (or indeed negative) behaviours. Should young people behave *regardless* of how well or poorly they are being taught, in a 'do as you are told' way of thinking about learners, or are they entitled to react to what is going on in their classrooms? This is not to *excuse* poor behaviour or to say that it *always* has a deeper meaning – sometimes, perhaps quite frequently with teenage learners, it is just kids being kids. But to suggest that a system alone should do all the work of managing behaviour is to downplay the skill of teachers and our own role in the success of the learning and behaviour that happens in our classrooms.

If you think for a moment about your *own* behaviours as a learner, you might have noticed that you are more likely to 'misbehave' in a CPD (continuous professional development) session if it does not make sense to you or if you feel like it is boring, irrelevant or just poorly presented. As an adult, you can probably get away with what teachers might call low-level misbehaviours by being subtle about them – sneaking out your phone to use on your lap or whispering with a friend. If we extrapolate from this to our own teaching situations, it is hard to maintain the idea that children and young people *should just behave*, given that even as adults we can be poor at it. My training work regularly brings me into contact with large groups of adults – sometimes 500 or more. Even though I am working with professional educators, who fully understand how inappropriate behaviour can make them feel, I still need to establish an expectation of 'one voice' at the start of my sessions. If I do not, well-qualified professionals will sometimes behave in a way that we would judge 'rude' in our learners, mainly because it is just normal human behaviour to push the boundaries.

A shift in our thinking can help us to figure out the self-regulation skills that a learner has not yet mastered or help us to find explanations for the tricky behaviours that we experience. For instance:

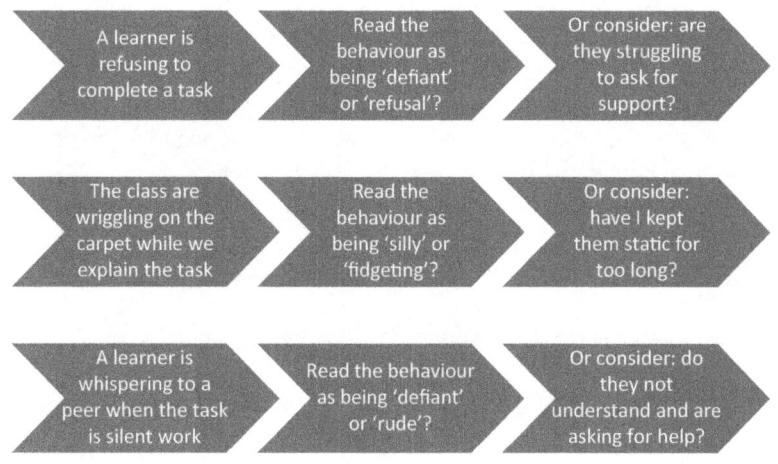

By trying out the alternative way of thinking about behaviour in each of these scenarios, *before* we assume that the behaviour is just communicating 'this learner is behaving poorly and being rude', we are far less likely to get into confrontations. Misunderstandings are completely natural and normal in a classroom, so asking 'Do you need a bit of support to get started?' or 'Is there something you need a bit of help with?', rather than reaching immediately for sanctions or a negative reaction, should help us to achieve a better result. Your learners may be taken aback a bit by your questions and assume that you are being sarcastic (and indeed, there might be an element of this). But the reality is that we are more likely to get a positive result if we check for misunderstandings or difficulties before we start doling out sanctions or consequences.

The idea that classroom behaviours can act as feedback allows teachers to interact with, interpret and respond to behaviours as more than just a problem that needs to be solved, but instead as a communication that can be 'read'. This is one of the questions that I have about pedagogical approaches where all the learners in a class are expected to position their bodies in a particular way. These techniques are usually combined with an acronym that indicates a specific set of body movements that should be made by all the learners simultaneously ('track me'). But this imposes a form of communication on learners that might mean that we miss some of the underlying cues – for instance, internal confusion or upset. It presumably also creates a heavy cognitive load for them. Mainly, though, if we want self-regulation to come from inside, rather than via extrinsic factors, we have to allow learners to strive for appropriate behaviours *themselves*.

An example of what co-regulation is

A useful story that I use, which explains what co-regulation looks like, is about the forest club that takes place weekly at our Early Years setting. To get to the forest area where the outdoor learning takes place, the children must climb up a steep, muddy bank. This is challenging when you are only small. When the children first come to forest club, they stand at the bottom of the bank, hold up their hands and plead with staff to 'pick me up!'. If we were to pick them up and put them at the top of the bank, this would be us doing all the work of regulating for them. There would be no co-regulation, no sense of challenge and no self-regulation. So, what we do instead, is:

✓ Give them a little physical boost to help them to get going up the slope.
✓ Let them know that we believe in them by saying, 'That's it, I know you can do it!'

> - ✓ Have one practitioner at the top of the slope and another at the bottom guiding them, to help them to feel safe and supported.
> - ✓ Give them guidance and reassurance – 'Reach for that branch!', 'That's great!'
> - ✓ Let them know when the challenge is almost complete – 'Nearly there now!', 'Almost made it to the top!'
> - ✓ Praise their resilience after the event, ensuring that we highlight how they stuck at it and kept going.
>
> Essentially, what our staff are doing is using the same scaffolds and supports that you might use for any area of the curriculum to differentiate or adapt your teaching to meet everyone's learning needs.

Thinking about co-regulation

Co-regulation begins from a baby's very earliest days, when a parent or carer rocks them to help soothe them. Gradually children learn to do what is called 'self-soothing': to calm themselves when they feel upset – for instance, sucking a thumb or rubbing a cloth or toy. Essentially, all these actions are aimed at rebalancing the baby or child's sensory system. Scientists have recently discovered something called 'mirror neurons', which are neurons that respond to actions that we see in others. We can encourage our learners' brains to mirror our actions by demonstrating what we do to calm ourselves down. In other words, by modelling self-calming strategies, we support learners to self-regulate themselves.

The term 'co-regulation' essentially means the scaffolds and supports that adults offer children to gradually help them learn how to regulate their own emotions and behaviours. Essentially, we are regulating *alongside* the child, gradually decreasing the levels of support until the child can manage for themselves. Most of the time these scaffolds will be put in place as learning happens to support the learner, and we then gradually increase the child's level of independence with the task or skill – in other words, what we might think of as keeping them in the 'zone of proximal development', as described by the educational theorist Vygotsky (1978). However, sometimes you will need to help a learner to co-regulate when they have *lost* emotional control and are having what we might call a 'meltdown'. It is better, if possible, to avoid learners getting into a totally dysregulated state. By this point, their brains will be in 'fight or flight' mode, and there will be no hope of rational discussion until they have calmed down. At the same time, it is worth remembering that occasionally an emotional 'meltdown' can be cathartic and help you to cope with difficult emotions. We need to be careful not to confuse having an emotional outlet with being dysregulated.

The scaffolds or supports that we use can take a variety of forms, depending on the age of the child and our relationship with them (i.e. a parent can soothe a child in different ways to a teacher; it will be natural for an Early Years practitioner to physically comfort a child, but this is not appropriate if you are working with teenagers). Sometimes the situation will require some kind of physical 'boost' (for instance, a child struggling to complete a difficult task outdoors) and other times it will require an emotional 'boost', such as comforting or calming the child. The older children become, the more you probably need to take a 'hands-off' approach in supporting them to get their emotions back under control.

Some useful scaffolding-type co-regulation strategies include:

- ✓ giving them a little physical 'boost' – for instance, if they are struggling to climb an obstacle
- ✓ using encouraging phrases, such as 'you can do it' or 'I know you can manage this', if they seem blocked in their learning
- ✓ letting them know that you will come back to support them again in a moment, to give them a sense of security.

Some useful emotional co-regulation strategies include:

- ✓ soothing a young child by rubbing their back, giving them a hug or a cuddle
- ✓ quietly speaking to the child, letting them know that you are there and things will be OK
- ✓ encouraging the young person to breathe deeply in and out (often we start to hyperventilate when we are upset, sucking in too much oxygen but not breathing it out again).

When a child is dysregulated, i.e. they have lost regulatory control, there is no point in trying to reason with them – you may have seen this when a young child has an emotional outburst or what some people might call a 'tantrum'. In this kind of situation, the first step is to help the child to get regulated again, and you can help them to do this simply by relating to them – letting them know that they are not alone, that you are there and that you care about them. It is only once they are relatively calm that it is worth trying to think things through by talking through what happened and thinking about how to avoid it happening again – in other words, the rational reasoning and reflecting that we might do after a situation has happened, to try to avoid it occurring again.

Ideally, we want to keep learners in a calm, alert but responsive frame of mind. We need to avoid triggering what is referred to as the 'fight or flight' response, where a learner goes into panic mode. At this point, they are highly unlikely to be able to access their rational brain and calm themselves back down without the support of an adult. The American psychiatrist B.D. Perry (2024) describes this using a spectrum of potential emotions:

Thinking things through

As we saw in the previous chapter, language is an essential aspect of self-regulation because it allows us to 'think through' our ideas and actions before they happen or while they are taking place. When a teacher gives a child a series of instructions, the child must hold those instructions in what is referred to as their 'working memory', in order to work through them and follow them. Without language, this is tricky (although not impossible) to do. When we co-regulate, we essentially help our learners to 'think things through' by supporting their thinking, and this often involves language. However, we can also help learners to 'think things through' by using other ways of making meaning – for example, using visuals, diagrams and concrete hands-on resources. These approaches support and enhance verbal/linguistic communication, enabling children to interpret, understand and 'hold onto' more ideas than they might otherwise be able to do.

Similarly, thinking things through together with a learner is part and parcel of the technique of co-regulation. Essentially, by narrating the situation for them, we are showing learners how it is possible to think through our emotions and reactions and figure out what to do about them. We might say something like 'I can see that you are getting frustrated' or 'I sense that this is difficult for you', to help a child to identify their emotional state. We can also add in some thoughts about coping mechanisms – for example, by saying, 'When I start to get frustrated, I check to see whether I'm clenching my fists and if I am, I unclench them' or 'When I'm finding something really difficult to cope with, I find it helps to step away from the activity for a moment'.

Practical strategies for the classroom

When we think about behaviour as communication, a great starting point is to consider how we as educators talk about our learners' behaviour. Challenge yourself around the way in which you discuss behaviour, becoming more aware of how what you say might be interpreted (or misinterpreted) by your learners or others. Remember that the way in which you frame what you say will have an impact on your learners' sense of self and their belief that they have the power to change the way that they behave.

Be aware that the process of moving your learners from co-regulation to self-regulation is likely to be a long one, involving repeated scaffolding and support to help them 'learn how' to regulate. Remember that this process is developmental, requiring changes in their brains to better be able to behave, pay attention, control impulses and so on. Even once learners have built their self-regulation skills, they may succeed or fail in managing to regulate from day to day (just as we do as adults), particularly when stress levels are high or emotions are heightened. One of the keys to success is providing sufficient agency and challenge for your learners to develop these skills – we cannot learn to co-regulate without that push to stretch and improve ourselves. Another key way in which children and young people develop these skills in school is through the repeated modelling of what a calm, regulated approach to handling tricky situations looks like. Every time you handle inappropriate behaviour in your classroom, you are providing a great example of this.

- ✓ Demonstrate that you can stay calm, no matter the provocation. Children pick up on the emotions and behaviours of the people around them, so model calm behaviour as much as possible.
- ✓ Avoid using words that make a judgement on behaviour, such as 'silly', 'lazy' or 'can't be bothered'. Stick to objective, descriptive terms instead – describe the behaviours that you observe.
- ✓ Try to start interactions with an offer of support, rather than a demand for action or an insistence that you will need to apply punitive measures.
- ✓ Focus on statements about what you *do* want, rather than what you *do not* want. So, instead of saying something like 'Stop being so silly, Sam', you might say, 'Sam, I need you to pick up your pen and start writing now.'
- ✓ Describe the emotions that you see on children's faces and what you think they might be communicating – for instance, saying 'I can see from your face that you seem to be getting upset.'
- ✓ Take a metacognitive approach, asking learners to 'think about where these emotions are coming from and how you could handle them'.
- ✓ Consider different ways in which to calm down, and practise these with your learners. This can be very individual – one learner might find that sipping water calms them down, while another might find that breathing deeply or listening to music has the same effect.
- ✓ Offer resources that will help children and young people to communicate and regulate their emotions – for instance, a teddy that they can hug if they are

upset, a cushion that they can hit if they are frustrated, or a balloon that they can blow up to rebalance their breathing when they are hyperventilating.
- ✓ Praise successful examples of learners demonstrating self-regulation, particularly after an episode where a young person has become dysregulated – for instance, saying 'You should be really pleased with the way that you handled your feelings there and calmed yourself down.'

Part Two

Supporting the Development of Self-Regulation in the Classroom

Chapter 4
Managing My Behaviours

In this chapter, we will:

- ✓ Consider how behavioural control develops during early childhood.
- ✓ Think about what we mean when we talk about 'poor behaviours'.
- ✓ Explore the skills that our learners need to develop in order to understand and control their behaviour.
- ✓ Examine ways in which we can pre-empt tricky behaviours before they arise.
- ✓ Understand the role of proprioception in self-regulation and classroom behaviour.
- ✓ Consider why routines are so important and how they support behaviour.
- ✓ Identify key strategies for pre-empting and handling behaviour in the classroom.

This chapter examines how teachers can support children and young people to become aware of their own behaviours, to understand why they might be behaving as they are and, consequently, to better manage their behaviours. Understandably, there is a tendency in education to lean into whole-school systems to help us to manage behaviour. These systems have plenty of benefits – not only do they help to ensure consistency in terms of expectations and responses to positive and negative behaviour, but they also give teachers a structure to use in their classrooms to help them ensure that the best possible teaching and learning can take place. Behaviour systems give young people and their families information about the school's expectations and how they can aim to meet these. However, the problem with systems comes when we lean on them too heavily. We start to expect the system to do the work for us, instead of remembering that the teacher – and their relationship with the learners – is one of the key factors within the system that makes it work.

We need to help our learners understand what their behaviours are, the impact that their behaviours have on others and that they can and should make more positive choices around this area of their lives. By getting them to think about what triggers certain behaviours and why they are problematic in a classroom situation, we support them in developing impulse control and other key self-regulation skills. When we spend time narrating the *purpose* of the behaviours that we ask for in class, rather than simply trying to impose them, we are, in turn, more likely to get our learners to behave as we need. When exploring this area of the subject of behaviour, it is worth asking yourself whether you always behave perfectly in every situation, and if not, why not? What is it that motivates you to act respectfully and cooperatively, and what causes those moments where you do not?

If we view behaviour as part of teaching and learning, rather than as separate from it, we can see that we are teaching our learners how to behave *as learners*, as well as how it might be best to behave *as people*. One of the issues with heavily behaviourist approaches to managing behaviour is that it can be tempting to 'jump' to the system too quickly. We might immediately start to apply sanctions and ask to have learners removed. This could be partly because there is too much difficult behaviour for us to handle, but also because we have been told to 'use the system' to manage the problem. Unfortunately, this can mean that we miss out on the low-level, small and subtle interventions, such as giving scaffolds or using non-verbal communication, that mean that we do not have to call on the system so frequently. This chapter explores what some of those interventions might look like.

The development of behavioural control

In many ways, this entire book is about the 'development of behavioural control'. The following chapters look at the different aspects of self-regulation that combine to become what we might call 'good behaviour' in a school context. Self-regulation is essentially an umbrella term for all the factors that go together to make up what we refer to as 'behaviour': impulse control, emotional regulation, empathy, resilience, goal setting, attentional control, motivation and so on. Ask any teacher to identify why some learners behave inappropriately while others do not, and they will often talk about issues with 'the home'. Perhaps we sometimes underestimate how difficult being a parent can be – knowing how to set and stick to clear boundaries, understanding how language develops, even just having the time and financial position to give your energy to your child – these are not necessarily simple to achieve.

In their earliest years, babies do not 'control' their behaviours – it is important for their survival that they are 'needy' because a baby's cry expresses that they need something from their caregivers. Interestingly, a baby's cries are effectively designed by nature to be impossible to ignore – what we might call the ultimate attention-getting behaviour. A baby's mental development occurs in an interplay with their carer or carers – where adults are emotionally responsive and attuned to their baby's needs, this creates a sense of security and strong attachment. Parents and carers are modelling for their babies and young children the entire time they are with them – this is what relationships look like, this is what love looks like, this is what being kind looks like and so on. As they become mobile, toddlers start to act on their desire to control and change their environment. They become more goal-directed than they were as babies and they can usually start to comply with simple requests (or, in other words, do what teachers would call 'behave').

However, young children easily get frustrated and will often resist caregivers' requests for specific behaviour. It is only as their brains develop further that they become more able to manage their frustrations or distress. Aggression has been shown to peak at around two years old (Chang et al., 2015), and many parents or Early Years practitioners will recognise the oppositional behaviours that sometimes get called the 'terrible twos'. In their third year, children typically start to be able to understand boundaries and to handle more difficult self-regulatory challenges. They begin to be able to inhibit some of their impulses and wait for what they want. Clearly, the complexity of the way in which what we call 'behaviour' develops in children is influenced by numerous factors. Not only is this about bonds and relationships with caregivers, but the development of children's behaviour can also be affected by issues such as malnutrition, stress, genetics and so on.

Definitions of behaviour

Before we start to think about how we can encourage young people to control their behaviours, it is worth thinking about what we mean when we talk about 'poor', 'difficult' or 'inappropriate' behaviours in the first place. The kinds of low-level behaviour that get in the way in a classroom situation are typically an inability or unwillingness to listen, a lack of focus, off-task behaviours and negative peer group interactions. When we think about behaviour from the perspective of self-regulation, we can see that many of these behaviours are skills that fall under this wider umbrella. For instance, children need to be able to control their impulses in order to avoid 'calling out' the answers during a Q&A session. Young people need to be able to filter distractions and maintain their concentration in order to be able to sustain their focus on learning and what the teacher is saying. By coming at the issue from the perspective of 'what skills do they still need to learn?', as well as 'how can I get them to follow the rules?', we give ourselves more options to support our learners' development.

Of course, it is not necessarily possible to both teach the curriculum and spend time teaching behaviour skills, especially with an increasingly crowded school day.

Interestingly, though, these skills form part of *what is taught* in the Early Years in England, where self-regulation makes an appearance under 'personal, social and emotional development' as a prime area within the early learning goals. When we examine the science behind child development, we can see that the changes in the brain that support increased impulse control (and other skills such as empathy and focus) do not happen only within a learner's earliest years. This is especially so for those learners from backgrounds where there has been trauma, high levels of stress and/or where boundaries have not been established and maintained. We cannot expect all our learners to have fully developed their self-regulation skills when we know how much the brain changes during childhood, adolescence and early adulthood.

On a practical level, teachers need to get on with teaching the curriculum and managing behaviour to the extent that the class as a unit is not disadvantaged by it. You can find lots of practical advice about strategies for positive behaviour management in my book *Getting Your Class to Behave* (2024). At the same time, if we can also learn to see 'poor behaviours' from the perspective of 'what skills do we still need to teach them?', as well as ask 'how can we use clarity of expectations and extrinsic motivators (sanctions, rewards) to get them to cooperate?', we give ourselves a wider set of options. Taking this approach also helps us to put the appropriate scaffolds in place to support learners and adapt our teaching to better meet their needs. We can start to pre-empt the problematic behaviours before they occur, by putting in place strategies that will help the learners to focus on the right thing. For instance:

- ✓ Where we know that a child is likely to get to the point of sensory overload in a busy classroom, leading them to lash out or shut down, we can put in place strategies before the overload occurs. This might mean the learner being given headphones to use to block out excess noise, or being encouraged to take a short 'brain break' before the sensory overload becomes too much – reasonable adjustments, in other words.

- ✓ If a primary class is always noisy and over-excitable when we ask them to get into a line to go to assembly, we might introduce an imaginative context – for example, asking them to 'imagine there is a giant asleep under the floor, and we don't want to wake him, so we need to tiptoe into our line'. This approach always reminds me of the classic parenting advice to 'hide the vegetables in the pasta sauce' – hide the behaviour that you want in an imaginative focus.

By encouraging children to focus on the specifics of how we need them to behave, encouraging the required behaviours by taking pre-emptive action or using an imaginative focus, we should be able to encourage more of the behaviours that we need and fewer of the behaviours that we do not.

The influence of proprioception on classroom behaviour

The term 'proprioception' describes our ability to know what our bodies are doing in space – to sense movement, action and location. This skill is made possible by proprioceptors, which are mechanosensory neurons located within our muscles, tendons and joints. Proprioception is the skill that allows us to close our eyes and touch a finger to our nose without having to see where our nose is to do so. Children and young people with a poorly developed sense of proprioception tend to use their bodies in ways that are typically interpreted as 'poor behaviours'. For instance, they might crash into others, hang off things, push, grab and shove, because they do not have the sensory information to know what their bodies are doing and how to use them more carefully. Children and young people with a slow response to proprioceptive information might also use too much or too little force – for instance, when writing. You might typically see these learners lean on things, slump in their chairs or be quick to tire because their muscles are weak and underdeveloped.

The proprioceptive input that we receive from our bodies can help us to calm and organise our brains. Those children who find this difficult to do need help to create a more efficient 'body map' so that they can use their bodies in a more appropriate way in a classroom context. Occupational therapists advise that you can help children and young people to develop their proprioception by using what is called 'heavy work'. This involves activities such as:

- ✓ digging
- ✓ carrying heavy items
- ✓ pushing
- ✓ hanging from bars.

In addition, you can use oral activities to help learners to develop a better sense of what their bodies are doing and calm their brains. These include actions such as:

- ✓ chewing
- ✓ crunching
- ✓ blowing bubbles
- ✓ blowing up balloons.

All these activities will help learners develop a stronger sense of what their bodies are doing, how much force they are using and where their bodies are in space. They will also provide the proprioceptive input that helps to calm the brain.

> ### An example of using proprioceptive information
>
> A teacher recently shared with me a lovely example of using proprioceptive input to support self-regulated behaviours. They had discovered that one of their learners with SEND (special educational needs and disabilities) had a particular interest in food. This was not because they were hungry, but because it helped them to manage sensory inputs and cope with sensory under- or overload. The teacher explained how they discovered that giving the young person a carrot to crunch on just before breaktime allowed them to 'hear the crunch' in their head. This, in turn, encouraged them to be energised and 'let off steam' during playtime. On returning to class, eating something soft helped them to calm back down. These are the kinds of possibilities that we might miss if we focus too closely and inflexibly on 'following the rules'. While eating food in class might lead to sanctions in a typical school behaviour policy, making this simple adjustment allowed a learner with SEND to cope and thrive.

Why routines matter

Every teacher understands the importance of routines in the classroom, but it is worth considering what it is that makes these so helpful, particularly in relation to self-regulation. For a start, routines help the learners to know what to expect and how to meet the teacher's expectations because the repetition of the routines helps to embed the agreed behaviours. This gives children and young people a sense of security – they know what to expect because it has been expected on numerous occasions previously. Routines are very helpful for the teacher as well – they mean that you can rest your voice from time to time, such as during the first and last part of a lesson, when your learners are completing their entry or exit routine without the need for your verbal inputs.

An interesting aspect of routines is that routines or habitual actions are stored in a different part of the brain (the basal ganglia) to aspects such as decision-making and attentional control (the prefrontal cortex). By creating clear routines that the learners can follow without having to think too much about them, they have less information to process in order to complete the actions. This frees up their concentration and attention for other things. In addition, having a clear routine also means that learners can get into good habits and the teacher can praise them for remembering to do these things. Routines build social norms that create a positive feedback loop – when all your peers are following the routine, it starts to feel like something that you all simply do as effective learners.

It can be tricky for some learners, especially those who have working memory or language processing difficulties, if the teacher gives a general instruction, such as 'get ready to go home'. The instruction is too vague: there is not enough detail to 'hold onto' for the learner to follow the instructions. Aim to be clear and explicit about exactly what it is that you need your learners to do, rather than using generalised commands. For instance: 'First, please put your pen in the pot, then put your book in the tray, and finally put your lunch box in your bag.' We can practise routines so that our learners get used to them, challenging them to complete the routine more efficiently each time they do so. We should also be open to adapting or changing routines where necessary, if an aspect of what we are doing appears to be problematic or less effective.

Agency and routines

At the same time as acknowledging the importance of routines, it is also useful to remember that excessive structure is not necessarily helpful. It can encourage us to effectively 'turn our brains off' and stop processing what we are doing. I heard a good example of this recently. A teacher told me that they had been asking children to put their book bags into a specific box every morning, depending on the reading level that they were on. When one day the boxes had been arranged in a slightly different order, the children continued to put their bags into the box that was in the same *position*, but which was now the wrong box.

In life, we must often deal with the unexpected, and we need to be careful not to get our learners so habituated that they don't really have to think during the routines that we use. The evidence around self-regulation suggests that children and young people need to learn to cope and adapt, as well as to fall into familiar patterns. Research (Barker et al., 2014) seems to show that overly structured activities may lead to a decrease in self-directed executive functioning. Where adults organise too many aspects of a learner's experiences, the lack of agency that learners feel can result in them mentally 'handing over' control to the adults. Overly structured approaches can also give children and young people too much scaffolding, with the result that they may struggle when life throws up unexpected challenges. For this reason, it is useful to 'change things up' and give your class some challenges that they did not anticipate from time to time, or to tweak aspects of the routine.

It is useful to enable learners to feel some sense of agency within routines by asking them to make decisions and choices. These can be at a simple level, with a learner being asked to choose between two different options, i.e. with the teacher scaffolding the options rather than offering unlimited choices. To add a sense of agency and decision-making to your routines, you can incorporate simple choices, such as:

- ✓ a choice between two different starter activities
- ✓ a decision when self-registering, e.g. milk or water for snack-time
- ✓ a choice of a new book to take home to read
- ✓ an activity to decide which emotion they are feeling, from a small range of choices
- ✓ a 'chilli choice' of tasks from which to pick, ranging from 'cool' (green) to 'hot' (red) with 'cool' tasks being simpler/easier ones and 'hot' tasks being more challenging.

Practical strategies for the classroom

A key starting point for getting your learners to reflect on and improve their behaviours is to spend time narrating the behaviours that you see and what these behaviours tell you about your learners. It is important and useful to frame what you see in terms of choices because this supports the development of a sense of agency, which, in turn, is so crucial in building self-regulation skills. Your aim should be to encourage children and young people to believe that their behaviours belong to *them*, and that consequently they can decide to do things differently if they really want. To encourage this sense of agency for your learners, ensure that you:

- ✓ Talk about behaviour in terms of choices – for instance, saying 'Let's see who's chosen to settle quickly down to work' or 'That's great, you've made the decision to get straight onto task'.
- ✓ Frame decisions about individual behaviour as a choice that the learner can make. For example, if a learner is refusing to work, you can say: 'You need to get on with your work. If you get on with it now, in class, that's great because I'm here to support you.'
- ✓ Where a learner continues to refuse to cooperate, describe any consequences as an alternative that is being chosen – for instance, saying, 'Unfortunately, if you choose not to do it in class, I will be left with no option but to ask you to complete it at home/in detention.'
- ✓ Do not put learners on the spot over this – some take-up or thinking time is required. Simply say, 'I'll give you a chance to think about that and come back to you in a little while. Make a good decision.'
- ✓ When you return to check on the decision that the learner has made, hopefully you can praise them for making a good choice. If not, explain that you will have to follow through with the consequences.

A useful tip when giving instructions to learners who tend to react with defensiveness or defiance is to offer two options from which to choose, rather than making a direct demand. This helps them to feel a sense of agency rather than perceiving themselves as being trapped into doing something. It is a particularly useful strategy for learners with SEND, such as pathological demand avoidance (PDA). For example, you might say, 'Would you prefer to start by doing X, or would you rather start by doing Y?'

Focus on the positive

Instinctively, when we face inappropriate behaviour, we tend to focus on the negative. Perhaps the most important strategy of all for supporting behaviour change is to be aware of this tendency in yourself and to work to overcome it. Even if it feels a bit 'fake', make sure that you spot, highlight, talk about and praise those learners who are doing the *right thing*. It is worth actively pushing yourself to do this; setting a target can work well to ensure that you remember. The evidence seems to suggest that a ratio of around five positive comments to every one negative comment is about right. *Before* you intervene to deal with inappropriate behaviour (unless it is obviously and immediately dangerous), get into the habit of shining a light on all the learners doing the right thing. Your positive comments might be something like:

- ✓ 'Thanks Aisha, that's great, you made the choice to get straight down to work' for an individual.
- ✓ 'It's lovely to see that this table has made the right choice and is ready to listen and learn' for a group of learners.

Teachers often describe to me the frustrations of trying to get a whole class silent before they can get on with teaching. When a class really is not settling but there are some learners who clearly just want to get on with the lesson, it can work well to go and sit with those learners. Start to have a chat with them about how frustrating it must feel for them and how you can see that they just want to get on with learning but are having to wait for their peers. Praise them, thank them and shower them with compliments, and what you should find is that many of the others in the class pick up on this and start to fall silent as well.

Achieving unconditional positive regard

A great way in which to help your learners to separate themselves from their behaviour, and consequently believe that they have the power to change it, is to describe behaviours as external to the person doing them. In other words, what you are effectively saying to them is 'You are not your behaviours, you can choose to change them' and 'No matter how you behave, I will continue to support you to improve yourself'.

To help to achieve this separation between the person and their behaviour:

- ✓ Talk about the behaviour and its consequences (not in terms of sanctions, but in terms of 'real life' outcomes), encouraging learners to think things through – for example, 'When we don't take care of the resources, what do you think might happen? That's right, they could get broken.'
- ✓ Describe the behaviour and why it is problematic, using 'we' rather than 'you' to depersonalise it, i.e. 'when behaviour x happens, this means y'. For instance, you might say: 'When we don't take care of the resources, they can get damaged and then we don't have any resources to use.'
- ✓ Make it clear that you care about and value your learners, and that this is not linked to any struggles that they may have to behave appropriately. Help them to understand that although the behaviour may be difficult and disappointing, it does not change your view of them as someone of value.
- ✓ Aim to reboot your opinion of and feelings towards learners every time you meet them, making it explicit to them that this is what you are doing. This might be something as simple as a positive comment when they arrive with you that day, such as 'I'm really looking forward to what you are going to achieve today', or even being more specific and saying, 'I'm hoping we can put aside yesterday's situation and start with a blank canvas today.'
- ✓ Avoid using words that prejudge behaviours by labelling the person – for instance, using words like 'silly' or 'lazy'. Where we label a child or young person, this can negatively influence our interactions with them, including on a subconscious level. Words that ascribe a motivation to a behaviour to judge it tend to encourage us to link the behaviour to the learner – as in 'They're just a silly child' or 'They're always lazy when it comes to maths'.
- ✓ It is helpful to try to avoid using these types of words to describe behaviour even when you are not in the classroom and the learners cannot hear you saying them – for instance, when talking about a young person in a staff meeting or during a CPD session.
- ✓ Look behind the labels that you feel tempted to use when describing learners to others, to identify the actual, observable behaviour. This will help you to find solutions to what might feel like intractable problems. For example, if you say something like 'They never complete the task' or 'They only write a few words', rather than 'They can't be bothered to do the work', this encourages you to figure out *why* the task-avoidant behaviours are happening.

Of course, demonstrating unconditional positive regard does not mean that we are not entitled to feel upset or cross when our learners behave inappropriately or exhibit really challenging behaviours in class. It is perfectly understandable and justifiable to feel affected by it, and sometimes to feel angry about it. Our emotions are just as valid as the emotions of our learners; it is just that we are better able to self-regulate and control them because we are adults and professionals being paid to do just that. At the same time, though, it typically works best not to *show* those emotions to the learner, so if possible save your emotional reaction for when the learners are not in the room. (Just think about how you felt when your own teachers reacted angrily when you were at school.)

Depending on the behaviour and the context, it is important to put in place a consequence that makes it clear that the behaviour is not acceptable. It can help to minimise stress by learning to distance ourselves from the inappropriate behaviour and its impact, by reminding ourselves that it is not the person that is the problem but the behaviour. This should hopefully help us to find it easier to cope with and manage.

Strategies for pre-empting problematic behaviours

A key focus for supporting children and young people to manage their own behaviours is to put in place strategies that pre-empt the most common problems that we experience. This, in turn, models for the learners the various ways in which adults can maintain calm and handle tricky situations, even when put under high levels of stress. The 'most common problems' will vary widely, depending on which phase or age group you work with, what kind of context your school is in and perhaps also which subject or subjects you teach. Consider whether it is possible to avoid behaviours occurring in the first place by putting a different approach in place that makes them less likely to happen. This could involve:

- ✓ adapting your classroom routines or approaches to support better behaviour
- ✓ adapting your curriculum provision to enable more successful outcomes for learners
- ✓ knowing what the triggers are for individuals and then intervening early, before the problem behaviours arise.

Ideally, it is better for us to stop learners from triggering what some people refer to as the 'reptilian' brain, i.e. becoming upset, overwrought, angry, aggressive and completely dysregulated, rather than having to mop up the emotional mess after it has occurred. By doing this, we should be able to create a calm, purposeful atmosphere, which, in turn, should make it less likely that further issues will arise. Pre-empting problems is about forward planning and lateral thinking. Sometimes it can take a bit of experimentation to find the right solution to the issue, and the best solution is not always the most obvious one. Ask yourself:

- ✓ What problems do I commonly experience with behaviour?
- ✓ When in the lesson (secondary) or the day (Early Years/primary) do these problems occur? (The answer is quite often that they occur either at the start or end of a lesson or day, when teachers and learners are tired or might have other 'baggage' to deal with.)
- ✓ What are the likely motivations of the children or young people when this happens?
- ✓ What was it that triggered the situation – what was the antecedent?
- ✓ What is going on *behind* the behaviour – which skills are missing that I might need to scaffold or support the learners to build?
- ✓ How might I distract the learners from the problem behaviour? Is it wisest to distract them or to support them to work through it?
- ✓ How could I move their attention away from what they are doing towards something more positive and purposeful?

Adapting routines/approaches

It is interesting that we think nothing of adapting our teaching methods when our learners are struggling to understand an aspect of the curriculum – for instance, by giving them some concrete manipulatives to explore a problem if they are struggling with an aspect of maths. However, when it comes to behaviour, we have a tendency to lean on systems and policies, seeing any adaptations as 'inconsistencies'. I like to use the term 'flexible consistency' to describe the concept that we can maintain a consistent *expectation* for all of our learners, at the same time as being flexible in the ways in which we go about achieving it. For instance, I can have the same expectation of 'ties should be done up properly' for all the learners in my secondary classroom, but with some learners, I will just need to make a quick verbal gesture to say 'sort out your tie' right at the start of the lesson, while with other learners I might be better having a quiet word about how I 'won't have to notice it if you sort it out quickly' once they have got down to work on a task.

If we are repeatedly facing a very similar issue – for instance, inappropriate behaviour on the carpet in a primary class, or during the exit from the room in a secondary class – it makes sense to consider whether there is something about the routine or the strategies that are triggering the issue. Could we adapt the way in which we approach this in order not to trigger the problem in the first place, particularly if it is part of our regular routines? When exploring adaptations, it is useful to ask yourself some questions about the self-regulation skills that you are trying to develop:

- ✓ What do we want the learners to focus on or pay attention to at this point in our daily routine?
- ✓ How can we move their attention to this aspect – what might motivate them to 'do the right thing'?
- ✓ What is the impulse that they are struggling to control and how can we help them to manage this impulse in a more appropriate way?
- ✓ How would I feel and behave in this situation – what aspects of self-regulation might I struggle with here?

A primary example of adapting teaching methods

To give a practical, real-life example that will resonate with many Early Years and primary teachers, in our setting, we were experiencing an issue with children squabbling over spaces during carpet time activities. Despite talking about 'kind hands', we were still seeing problems around negative peer group interactions, which, in turn, were interfering with the children's ability to concentrate and learn. Instead of giving consequences to the children who were behaving inappropriately or rewards to those who were doing the right thing, we talked about how we might resolve this situation in other ways.

- ✓ First, we analysed what was going on to figure out what was *motivating* the issue – or, in other words, what the behaviour was communicating.
- ✓ The issue seemed to be about the children wanting their 'own personal space' on the carpet and struggling to figure out how to achieve this.
- ✓ Thinking laterally, we wondered whether the problem was as much with the carpet as it was with the children themselves. How could we adapt the scenario, we wondered, so that the carpet was no longer a problem?
- ✓ We went to a carpet shop and were kindly given a set of samples of carpet tiles. These are individual, rectangular pieces of carpet in the shape of a small mat, which are given to customers (a bit like a tester pot of paint).

- ✓ We chose neutral colours such as greys and browns because we did not want to replace one issue (quarrels over carpet spaces) with another issue (quarrels over mat colours).
- ✓ We adapted our routine, adding a song to the mix to create a sense of energy and forward motion.
- ✓ Now, once all the children are registered, one of the learners rings a handbell to indicate that it is time to come to the 'carpet'.
- ✓ The children start singing 'find a mat, find a mat, find a mat, find a mat'. Then they all march over to the box of mats, take a mat for themselves and position it in the area where we do our carpet time activities.
- ✓ This genuinely seems to have stopped the arguing, elbows, wriggling and so on that had previously been a feature of this part of our routine.

Other ways in which teachers might adapt their carpet routines include giving children a cushion to sit on, having a carpet with squares where each child is given one square to sit on, and so on.

A secondary example of adapting teaching methods

Similarly, to give another real-life, practical example that should resonate with secondary teachers, a common problem that occurs in secondary classrooms is a noisy, chaotic end to lessons, as the learners pack their bags, push in their chairs and exit the room. This is often a time when school systems are not particularly helpful because the last thing that you want to be doing is handing out sanctions just as a class is leaving. Not only would this end the lesson with a negative atmosphere, but in addition it is unlikely to be practical or successful, as the learners are in a rush to get off to their next lesson.

When teaching in one London secondary school, I regularly had issues with the end of lessons, at least in part due to the nature of my classroom, which had two exits and so was a bit like a corridor in terms of its layout. In addition, space was tight, so inevitably learners would rub up against each other as they tried to gather up their belongings at the end of lessons. I decided to add a specific strategy/activity to finish off my lessons and to make learners feel calmer and more purposeful. In this instance, I was also able to incorporate an imaginative focus to the activity, which ended up becoming almost like a mindfulness exercise (back in the days before mindfulness was even a 'thing'). I ended up using this activity with both Key Stage 3 and Key Stage 4 learners, and it transformed the ends of my lessons.

- ✓ About five minutes before the end of the lesson, I explained to the class that I was going to ask them to 'freeze' still like statues. I framed this as a 'challenge' that I knew that they could achieve. I would then say 'three, two, one, freeze!' and the 'game' was to see who could freeze completely and totally still.
- ✓ There was an interesting correlation between those learners who struggled to self-regulate (although we did not use that term back in those days – we might have said something like 'fidget') and those learners who could simply not keep their bodies completely still. Looking back, those learners probably struggled with proprioception and impulse control.
- ✓ While the learners were 'frozen', I would give out reminders about homework, praise them for their learning and behaviour (if appropriate) and generally 'finish off' the lesson in a calm and quiet way.
- ✓ Just before the bell went for the end of the session, I would say 'three, two, one, unfreeze' and the challenge was then for them to tuck their chairs in under their desks but *in silent slow motion, like in a movie.*
- ✓ By putting their attention and focus on the 'in slow motion' idea, we were able to maintain the calm, considered end to the lessons, most of the time.
- ✓ I would also challenge each class to 'freeze' better and for longer than other year groups: 'Oh, Year 7 can freeze for two minutes, so I reckon you should be able to manage three minutes, Year 9.'

Again, by 'hiding the vegetables in the pasta sauce', I was able to get my classes to finish off the lessons in the manner that I wanted, without them really realising that this was what I was doing.

Adapting curriculum provision

For those of you who are working in the English system, 'the curriculum' is currently an extremely hot topic of conversation, not least because it is a key focus for Ofsted.

This puts it front and centre for schools, under the pressure of the accountability system that we currently face. We also see a focus on curriculum in Scotland and Wales, and clearly, it is an interesting and important part of the work that we do as educators. However, what seems to be happening is that curriculum is becoming increasingly pre-planned and inflexible – probably in reaction to Ofsted demanding that they see an 'appropriate sequence' for learning in different subjects. This, in turn, means that it is more difficult for educators and schools to be flexible around curriculum because inspectors want to see 'fidelity' to what has been planned.

Obviously, there are benefits to having a clearly pre-planned sequence of learning. Quite a bit of the time, one piece of learning does build upon another. It also means that everyone in a school should in theory know where the learners are, and if, for instance, there is a change of teacher, the pre-planned sequence can remain in place. Unfortunately (or perhaps fortunately), learning – and life – just does not always work like this. Sometimes, a learner will jump in their learning, apparently without following the 'correct sequence'. They will suddenly make three strides forward without us quite knowing what has happened to trigger this. Similarly, for other learners, trying to follow that exact sequence will be problematic, perhaps because of a gap in their prior experiences or because of a specific difficulty with learning or behaviour.

This, then, is a plea to consider your *curriculum provision* when issues around self-regulation crop up, rather than just considering your *policies* around behaviour. Some very important questions to ask ourselves in relation to our curricula include:

- ✓ Does this curriculum meet the needs of every child, and if not, whose needs is it not meeting?
- ✓ Is this curriculum equitable, fair and supportive of diversity or does it embed biases that we have, which we might not even be conscious of?
- ✓ Are we making reasonable adjustments to ensure that this curriculum, and the sequence in which it happens, is not disadvantaging learners with SEND but is actively supporting their progress instead?
- ✓ How does our approach to curriculum impact upon our teachers and other staff? Are we unnecessarily making life more difficult for them?
- ✓ Does the curriculum (or extra-curricular provision) offer sufficient outlets for some of the situations that threaten to overwhelm the learners – for instance, during playtimes?
- ✓ Is our behaviour policy impacting some learners much more than others, and are there ways in which we can adapt the curriculum to avoid this happening?
- ✓ Is our curriculum having unintended consequences, which, in turn, are impacting behaviour? For example, when learners have to stay static for long periods to complete a phonics session, is this, in turn, effectively 'causing' issues around inappropriate carpet behaviours?

> **An example of adapting curriculum**
>
> Again, to give a real-life example to illustrate the approach, about two years into the pandemic, we were having issues with behaviour in the afternoons in the Early Years setting that I help to run. We talked about our policy and whether we could utilise consequences to handle the situation. We also explored the possibility of introducing some extrinsic rewards (we have not used these in our setting for over a decade, and we were very reluctant to reverse this policy). In the end, we decided to revisit the curriculum itself and see what we might do to adapt that instead. We examined the times of day when behaviour began to deteriorate and noticed that this seemed to happen directly after lunch. Clearly, when you are working with young children, they start to get tired at this point, which can lead to difficulties with impulse control and a setting full of fractious learners.
>
> We decided that we would introduce a 'daily walk' into our timetable, so that the children had a chance to get out into the fresh air and exercise after lunchtime. Our daily walk also helps fulfil many aims of our curriculum because it supports physical development and learning about the natural world, as well as learning behaviours around road safety, building impulse control and other self-regulation skills. Our behaviour 'problem' has now effectively been 'solved', simply by considering what the children's behaviours might have been communicating to us.

Clearly, this solution is specific to our Early Years setting, and it might not be an answer for a large urban secondary school. However, it is worth asking ourselves about the role of curriculum and the need for it to flex to accommodate the development of self-regulation skills. If we rely on systems and policies, and this leads to the types of behaviour that cause us to suspend or exclude learners who cannot fit within that system, then considering how we might be more flexible can only be a benefit.

Avoiding the triggers

As well as pre-empting issues and adapting our approach or our provision, it is also possible to personalise our approach to individuals. This is particularly useful for those learners who have special needs. Where you know what tends to 'trigger' the child or young person, this can form part of making the legally required 'reasonable adjustments' to support their inclusion in class. Effectively, this is about empowering teachers to have knowledge about individual needs. If we are aware that a child in our care experiences sensory overload, then we can watch for the signs that the point of 'meltdown' is approaching.

If a learner starts to experience sensory overload in the time leading up to a break – for instance, when the lesson is too long for them to manage to sustain their attention – we might find a way in which to give them a quick 'brain break', i.e. a chance to move around and be physically active. For example, we could ask them to:

- ✓ take something to the office for us
- ✓ return an item to a teacher in another classroom
- ✓ step outside into the fresh air with a member of support staff
- ✓ collect equipment or resources
- ✓ wipe the whiteboard
- ✓ help to prepare some snacks for the class.

Giving them this opportunity to move around or to remove themselves from the room gives them a physical outlet and potentially time for a bit of space separate from their peer group. In turn, it may be that we completely avoid the situation where their behaviour deteriorates and they begin to go into 'meltdown'.

Chapter 5
Developing Impulse Control and Delayed Gratification

In this chapter, we will:

✓ Explore the way in which impulse control develops over time.
✓ Examine key protective factors that support the development of impulse control.
✓ Understand the issues that can impede impulse control.
✓ Learn more about the role of deferred or delayed gratification in long-term outcomes.
✓ Explore the concept of self-distancing and its influence on inhibitory control.
✓ Examine some key strategies for helping learners to regulate their impulses.

Impulse or inhibitory control is a key skill that our learners need to develop, particularly for when they are in the school environment. A classroom is a social context, where we must learn how to fit in, take turns and get along with others. A child who constantly snatches toys from others is likely to find it more difficult to make friends. A learner who repeatedly behaves in a defiant manner is likely to find themselves getting into trouble with staff. Our learners need to understand that they cannot always get what they want immediately, and that this is especially the case when they are in the school context. They will have to control the impulse to call out or to demand to get picked as a volunteer. Sometimes they will have to work hard in lessons when they do not feel like doing so. Children and young people need to learn how to cope with temporary difficulties, particularly where doing this can lead them to a better long-term outcome (what is referred to as 'delayed' or 'deferred' gratification).

As we saw in Chapter 1, the 'marshmallow experiment' (Mischel and Ebbesen, 1970) shows how impulse control – and the parallel skill of delaying or deferring gratification – is important in ensuring long-term positive outcomes. Although toddlers and even babies can start to control their impulses to a limited extent, this skill starts to properly develop at around the age of three years old. At this point, the prefrontal cortex, responsible for inhibitory control, becomes more active. With their developing grasp of language, children gradually start to understand social communication and societal expectations around how they are meant to behave, becoming more able to control those impulses. Some learners still really struggle with inhibitory control well into secondary school. Indeed, you can probably think of situations as an adult where a lack of impulse control proved to be problematic for you. This chapter looks at how impulse or inhibitory control develops and why it is more difficult for some learners than others to control their impulses. We also explore the vital role of delayed or deferred gratification in young people to help them focus on long-term goals over short-term ones.

The development of impulse control

The part of the brain that supports impulse control – the prefrontal cortex – is the slowest-developing brain region, and it continues to show changes through to adulthood. Like other self-regulatory skills, our lack of impulse control is part of an evolutionary survival mechanism designed to help us learn and develop with the guidance of adult carers. A baby will explore its world by reaching out to grab at things, with no understanding that this might or might not be a good idea. An adult will remove dangerous objects from reach or step in to remove them before the baby can get to them because the baby does not yet understand why they need to inhibit their impulse. When a baby is hungry, they will cry to communicate that they need to be fed; we would not want a baby to control this impulse to cry because we need to know when they are hungry and be alerted to this fact. On the other hand, an adult might feel the desire for food or actively feel hungry, but they could still manage to resist the impulse to eat something because of a longer-term goal (for instance, to reduce their refined sugar intake).

The parts of the brain that are associated with impulse control are immature at birth and only develop slowly through childhood. The prefrontal cortex is an important region in the development of self-control, with the orbitofrontal cortex being involved in decision-making as well. Another area of the brain that helps us balance logic and emotion is the anterior cingulate, which receives messages from many areas of the brain and integrates them to regulate our responses. This part of the brain becomes more active between three and six years, at which point children are better able to wait and control their impulses, gradually becoming more able to focus their attention, wait for a reward or share their toys.

Impulse control continues to develop throughout childhood and adolescence, with the brain areas involved in impulse control only becoming almost fully mature towards the end of the teenage years. Because their prefrontal cortex is still developing, teenagers tend to rely on a part of the brain called the amygdala to make decisions to a greater extent than adults do. This part of the brain is associated with impulses, emotions and aggression. This can lead to young people expressing very strong emotions and choosing riskier activities during their teenage years.

The way in which children are brought up in the earliest years can have a direct impact on their ability to control their impulses, with children who have adverse experiences being more liable to struggle to manage them. In addition, genetic factors can also have a significant impact on the development of these skills, with genes affecting the levels of dopamine in the brain. Similarly, environmental factors are also at play, with exposure to alcohol or drugs in the womb having the potential for negative impacts on impulse control. In addition, experiencing issues such as poverty and malnutrition during childhood can shape and influence the development of impulse control because these place additional stress on the child's developing body and brain.

Inhibitory control is what is known as a 'domain general' resource – we need to learn how to control our impulses in the varied domains of our behaviours, our emotions and our cognition. Impulse control is also a limited resource – it can easily get 'used up' when too many demands are made on us at any one time. When we are tired or under stress, we are likely to become less able to manage our impulses. Similarly, if we do not have access to adequate resources, such as food, we are going to be less likely to able to manage our impulses around them and more likely to struggle to share. Where a child is not sure whether there will be food on the table, the logical response that would help to ensure their own survival is to resort to grabbing or snatching behaviours.

Factors involved in the development of self-control

In a similar way to the development of many facets of self-regulation, secure attachments to a reliable caregiver are important in supporting the development of impulse control. Numerous studies (e.g. Berkman et al., 2012) have shown that adversity early on in life predicts poor impulse control in children. In turn, poor inhibitory control leads to other negative outcomes, including in academic functioning. At the same time, the long period of development of impulse control means that there is a lot of potential for interventions, particularly during the periods of brain plasticity associated with children's development.

Children living in poverty tend to be more prone to difficulties with self-control (Tarullo et al., 2009), and one potential factor here may be sleep disruption or deprivation. In an overcrowded household, where there is chronic stress, hunger and/or poor temperature control, or perhaps even the lack of a proper bed, it will be more difficult for children and young people to sleep properly. Tasks that involve the prefrontal cortex are sensitive to the amount of sleep that someone has had, so a poor night's sleep may lead to issues with impulse control the following day.

Interestingly, there is evidence to suggest that there are differences between genders in the ways in which self-regulation skills develop, with boys often experiencing a dip at around age two, while girls' self-regulation rises steadily. Some researchers have suggested that these differences in the developmental trajectories may be to do with cultural beliefs and expectations (Montroy et al., 2016). Girls are more likely to be expected to conform and comply, while boys are more likely to be encouraged to take risks and be confident.

For impulse control skills to develop, there needs to be a balance between responsiveness and supportiveness but also independence and agency in early approaches to parenting. Ideally, parents need to be sensitive and responsive to their young children, talking about emotions and other mental states, but also helping their children to develop autonomy and independence by allowing them to take managed risks and give things a go. By supporting children to have a try, with the knowledge that their caregiver will be there to help when they are struggling, they become better able to manage challenges, face difficulties and consequently control their impulses. Effectively, they need to practise getting it wrong, within a controlled environment, to eventually start getting it right.

Overly structured styles of parenting – what is sometimes called 'helicopter parenting' – can be problematic for the development of impulse control and associated self-regulatory skills. Indeed, many teachers will intuitively sense that this is so, as in a parent who over-helps their child – for instance, in hanging up their coat or completing their homework. Many of us can probably also recognise this impulse in ourselves in a classroom context, where we over-support learners because we think that it will help them to progress and avoid the emotional impact of failure. A recent study (Obradović et al., 2021) found that when parents stepped in more often during a task, to instruct, correct, make suggestions or ask questions, those children found it more difficult to self-regulate at other times. The children of these 'helicopter parents' also did less well on tasks measuring delayed gratification and impulse control.

With impulse control, it seems that it is possible to go too far the other way and to have 'too much of a good thing'. When children become over-controlled and never acknowledge or give in to their impulses, this in turn can interfere with healthy functioning. For instance, when a child is extremely shy, their high levels of self-control can be linked to being socially withdrawn and consequently less skilled at social communication. This seems to suggest that for a child to be socially skilled, as well as skilled at inhibiting their impulses, we need to encourage a mix of emotional reactions *alongside* supporting the development of inhibitory control. The healthy self-management of impulse control seems to mean knowing when to exert that control and when to loosen it up.

The importance of delayed gratification

Learning is typically hard-won: we need to stick at it, avoid the urge to give up, suppress the desire for a quick 'win' and keep going even when things get tough. Our aim as learners is typically to achieve a long-term goal (to learn to ride a bike, to speak a new language relatively fluently or to become a vet). To achieve this larger goal, we must delay or defer gratification and persevere. We will not get the positive feedback achieved from a successful end-result by refusing to go through the short-term discomfort of falling off a bike repeatedly, slogging to memorise new vocabulary or working hard to do well in our exams, for instance, so that we can progress to study veterinary medicine at university. The way that learning happens generally means that often we must sublimate our desire for a quick and easy 'win'.

As we saw in the first chapter of this book, the 'marshmallow experiment' (Mischel and Ebbesen, 1970) demonstrated how delayed gratification is closely correlated with positive long-term outcomes, particularly in education. This is because of the way in which the education system (and indeed learning itself) works – there are no short-term fixes. We must be willing to put in the hard work to get to a better end-result. The way in which the education system currently works leads to a situation where learners might be in a class of 30 or more children, studying something in which they have no interest at all. It is not possible in that context for everyone to get their own way simultaneously. We must learn to control the impulse to be the one who is the centre of attention, and to sublimate our own desires for the greater good of the class. This is perhaps why teachers find it so annoying when children shout out an answer – it immediately feels unfair to the child who has sublimated their need for attention and praise and who is sitting quietly waiting to answer with their hand in the air.

Various studies (e.g. Twito et al., 2019) have demonstrated that being able to delay gratification requires trust in the person offering you a greater reward. In a classroom situation, this would mean trusting your teacher to care about you and help you achieve better long-term educational outcomes. In these studies, a lack of trust led to children preferring the certain, immediate option, even though it offered a smaller gain. Similarly, where an educator is perceived as unreliable – for instance, where they are inconsistent in their expectations or they do not model the behaviour that they ask for – this is likely to make it more difficult for the learners to defer gratification.

Self-distancing and impulse control

The concept of 'self-distancing' is central to the development of impulse control. Evidence suggests that 'taking on a role' (i.e. viewing ourselves as 'someone else') can help us in regulating our behaviours, particularly where we need to persist at a task. What seems to happen is that this distancing allows us to manage our impulses because we are mentally at a distance from them. The same technique is also useful for developing empathy, where we mentally reposition ourselves in someone else's mind.

In a fascinating study exploring the phenomenon of self-distancing (White et al., 2017), children were asked to choose between completing a repetitive task and playing a video game. The aim was to 'stick at' the task rather than give in to the temptation to play the game. In the study, one group of children were asked to think about their own thoughts and feelings while they were doing the task ('Am I working hard?'); another group were asked to think about themselves in the third person ('Is Bea working hard?'); and a third group were asked to think about someone else who was good at working hard, picking from a group of well-known characters, including Batman, Bob the Builder and Dora the Explorer ('Is Batman working hard?'). The third group – who took on the mantle of the characters – were able to persist longer at the task, with the second group also more successful than the first.

One of the secrets to deferring gratification seems to be to mentally 'cool' the aspects of whatever it is that is tempting you – for instance, putting imaginary distance between yourself and the thing that you want to do. For example, imagining a treat as a picture instead of a real object helps children avoid the temptation to grab it. We can see in videos of children undertaking the 'marshmallow experiment' that some will literally remove themselves physically from temptation by sitting on their hands or moving themselves to the corner of the room. Others will stop looking at the marshmallow to enhance their willpower.

Interestingly, the concept of self-distancing seems to link to the mindfulness and meditation practices that also appear to be useful for developing self-regulation. These practices focus on the importance of stilling the mind and distancing oneself from worrying thoughts. Evidence (Kross and Ayduk, 2016) has shown that self-distancing is also helpful in allowing people to analyse negative experiences that they have had and in managing the emotional fall-out from these. The distancing appears to help them to focus less on the emotionally troubling features of the experience and more on thinking about it differently, to give them a sense of insight and closure. This, in turn, leads to fewer feelings of distress and less ruminating on the negative experience that we might have had.

The cycle of impulse control

The process model of self-control (Duckworth et al., 2016) demonstrates how impulses are generated and how they can be regulated, and as such, offers lots of food for thought for classroom teachers. This model describes impulse control as a cycle in which we react to a situation by paying attention to it, appraising it and then responding to it. The example given is of someone standing in a kitchen, seeing a box of doughnuts, thinking 'tasty treat!' and then eating one. There are various impulse control strategies that might help stop us from eating the doughnut at various points in the cycle – for instance, looking away from the doughnuts (as described in the technique of 'self-distancing') or hiding them to avoid seeing them. If you look for videos of 'the marshmallow experiment' online, you will see children looking at the ceiling, turning their backs on the treat and so on. Some sing to themselves or sit on their hands to help themselves control their impulses – these physical behaviours will be very familiar to many class teachers of young children.

The model suggests that there are five potential types of inhibitory control strategies that can be brought to bear on the situation. It is useful for educators to understand what these options are and to think about how they might already incorporate some of these as scaffolds for their learners, and what else they could potentially try.

- ✓ **Situation selection** means consciously choosing to be in places or with people who help us with our impulse control. For example, taking a route home where we avoid passing a cake or sweet shop could help us avoid the temptation to buy ourselves a sweet treat. For GCSE learners, studying in a library or café, rather than at home, might help them to better manage their attention because there are fewer potential distractions.

- ✓ **Situation modification** involves purposefully changing a physical or social situation that cannot be avoided – for instance, putting your alarm further away from your bed so that you must get out of bed to switch it off, thus making it more likely that you will not oversleep. In a classroom context, this might involve the learner asking to sit at the front, closest to the teacher, to avoid being distracted by their peers.

- ✓ **Attentional deployment** means strategically moving your attention away from the tricky aspects of your situation, to focus on something that will help you to maintain your impulse control – for example, helping a learner to focus on counting backwards to calm themselves rather than on their peer who is annoying them, when they are about to lose their temper.

- ✓ **Cognitive change** essentially means reframing a situation to think differently about it. An excellent example of this is in the acronym 'FAIL', which some teachers use to encourage learners to see failures as a 'first attempt in learning'. Another example could be breaking up a difficult task into smaller pieces to make it feel more manageable. This also links to self-distancing, where viewing the situation differently allows us to create space between ourselves and the impulse that we are facing.

✓ **Response modulation** is seen by researchers as the most straightforward technique, but also the least likely to be effective in the long term, particularly because it can generate negative emotional responses in the person. This approach would include impulse control strategies such as trying not to cry when we are sad or attempting not to smile when we find something funny.

Practical strategies for the classroom

There are plenty of opportunities in a classroom context to encourage children and young people to use and develop their self-control skills. Indeed, if we were to ask our learners, some of them would probably say that they are constantly being asked to control their impulses and that they would often rather be doing something else instead of being sat in class with us. One of the keys to supporting the development of impulse control is to find ways in which to hand the behaviour over to the learners, rather than always 'managing' it yourself. The impulse is situated within the learners themselves and, while we can put in place strategies to help them manage it, in the end, they must learn what it feels like to do this in order to be able to understand how it works for themselves. There are various techniques that you can use to 'hand over' the behaviour in your classroom. For example:

✓ Wait for silence, rather than calling for it, so the learners do the work of falling silent themselves.

✓ Get one of your learners to indicate when you need the class's attention – for instance, by ringing a bell for you.

✓ Use the 'secret student' technique, where you nominate one learner to look for examples of great behaviour from their peers.

✓ Incorporate strategies to encourage sharing, such as giving the learners a sand-timer to help them share a favourite resource. Once you have modelled using the timer to indicate 'I'm waiting', hand it over to the learners to manage the timings for themselves.

A key approach to supporting the development of impulse control skills is to encourage your learners to understand what it feels like to have an impulse but to wait to respond to it. Knowing what this sensation feels like is important in being able to replicate and reinforce it. Talk to your class about where in their bodies the sensation is felt, building their proprioceptive knowledge. Many common childhood games are fantastic vehicles for developing this understanding of impulse control in a classroom context. For example:

✓ In 'musical statues', you can see how this kind of game demands that we control our impulse to move in response to a 'stop' signal (the music stopping). In

Developing Impulse Control and Delayed Gratification

addition, we are required to remain still until the music restarts, so this game creates an internal proprioceptive focus on 'stilling' our bodies.

- ✓ An adaptation of this idea is the drama warm-up activity where learners move around the space and then 'stop' (freeze) and 'go' in response to a sound such as a drum beat.

- ✓ Where learners become adept at this stop/go activity, they can be challenged to move around the space and stop simultaneously as a group, *without anyone giving a signal*. They can then move off, again without anyone saying 'go'. Amazingly, it is perfectly possible for a whole class to do this once they get skilled at working as a 'unit'.

- ✓ Games can be used as part of a 'return to me' strategy for gaining the attention of a class – for instance, using 'Simon says' but changing the name to '[teacher] says'. This game is all about paying attention and following instructions, but also inhibiting an incorrect response (when the teacher does not say '[teacher] says'). Doing well at this game requires children to direct their attention and listen carefully to the instructions, while also inhibiting some of their impulses.

- ✓ Childhood favourites such as 'Grandmother's footsteps' or 'What's the time Mr Wolf?' also require high levels of impulse control. Children must not only move carefully and quietly, but they must also react quickly to 'freeze' and pay very close attention to do well in the game.

- ✓ Board games are another great example of impulse control because we must be able to take turns and cope with not winning. Often, these games require a fairly length period of waiting between turns, during which we need to give our attention to what other players are doing.

- ✓ Card games can also be supportive of impulse control. If you think about a simple game like 'snap', the players can feel that sensation of holding back from saying 'snap' but then having to react very quickly indeed when the moment arises to shout it out.

- ✓ The 'Ready ready' game, which we play in our setting, is another game that encourages the children to feel the impulse to react but to hold back from giving in to that feeling. The 'game' takes place once mat (carpet) time is finished, before the children move off to play in the environment. The teacher and the children say 'Ready, ready', while swinging their fingers in the air (as though conducting an orchestra) and then the teacher says 'Not just yet!' and the children must inhibit the urge to move. This is done several times, before the teacher finally says 'Ready to play!' and the learners can finally move.

It might feel like it would not be so feasible to incorporate these kinds of games into lessons with older learners, but in fact, they can be ideal as a way of structuring the end of lessons – for instance, the 'freeze like a statue' and 'slow motion tuck-in' challenge described in the previous chapter. Similarly, in subjects such as music or drama, many whole-class activities will effectively involve practising impulse control. For example, drumming to a beat that slows down and speeds up in a music lesson requires us to manage our impulses.

Supporting learners with ADHD

Learners who have attention deficit disorder (ADD) or attention deficit hyperactivity disorder (ADHD) will clearly find it much harder than their peers to inhibit their impulses. These learners have neurochemical and structural differences in their brain development, as well as lower levels of dopamine, meaning that they respond more immediately and reactively to their environment. Learners with ADHD typically find it much more difficult than their peers to sit still, to listen to instructions or to avoid 'blurting out' and interrupting the teacher. Learners with ADHD tend to act before they think and struggle to modify their behaviours based on discussions of future outcomes and consequences.

The adjustments that work best for learners who have ADHD tend to centre around pre-planning from the teacher to manage the environment, rather than responding to behaviours once they happen (O'Regan, 2018). Generally, these learners respond best when the environment:

- ✓ is well-structured, with clearly explained expectations
- ✓ is stimulating, with plenty of interest
- ✓ enables breaks for the learner to 'reboot' their impulse control levels
- ✓ minimises visual clutter and other sensory distractions
- ✓ offers plenty of rewards and positive feedback
- ✓ gives opportunities to move around.

In practical terms, this means incorporating strategies that will help many of your learners to focus and self-regulate, as well as supporting learners with SEND:

- ✓ Be explicit about the behaviours that you need, taking care to avoid generalised instructions. Rather than saying 'Tidy up your equipment', you might say something like 'Put your pens, pencils and rulers in your pencil case and then place it in your bag.'
- ✓ Agree a secret gesture with the learner to signal 'stay in your seat' or 'stop calling out', such as a low-key hand signal. This helps to avoid singling out the young person among their peers and reinforces the sense of you supporting the learner to manage their own behaviours.

- ✓ At times during the day or lesson that you know might 'trigger' impulsive behaviour, direct the learner to do something specific to channel their impulses – for example, to collect in the books for you or take something to the school office.
- ✓ Show the format of the day or lesson, either by using a series of images or by writing up your routine on the board. Refer regularly to where you are in the day/lesson to support the learner to cope with changing from one activity or lesson to the next. If you have written up your routine, the learner could wipe off each item as it is completed.
- ✓ Create an 'office' area for learners with ADHD by making a partition out of cardboard for them to put on their desks when they are working on a task. This allows the learner to manage distractions by blocking them out visually. It also gives them a space to help them to become more organised. For example, they could stick their daily timetable on the partition and cross off each part as they complete it.
- ✓ Offer visual reminders on cards for these learners to work through when they feel an impulse– for instance, a traffic light reminder card to 'STOP', 'THINK' and only then to 'DO'.
- ✓ Incorporate mindfulness or meditation activities to help your learners calm and still their minds while focusing on their bodies. These do not have to take up much time or be difficult to plan or manage – it might just be about having a calm piece of music playing as the learners enter the room.

With older learners, offer plenty of strategies to support exam revision and independent learning – for instance, teaching them the SMART acronym for effective goal setting (specific, measurable, achievable, relevant, time-bound) and how to apply this to their own learning. Work through some examples of smart goals – for instance, the best approaches for revising your subject. Help learners with drawing up timetables for revision and give them tips and advice to avoid procrastination.

Handling Q&As

A common issue for teachers is learners shouting out answers to questions. Clearly, this is an issue with inhibitory control, because the learner is not managing to control the impulse to share their vocal contribution. However, this is also the ideal situation for reflecting on and rethinking our approach to a very common classroom technique – a Q&A session with a class. There are plenty of strategies that teachers can use to support learners to better manage their impulses. Some of these are about incorporating additional scaffolds to help learners act sensibly during Q&As; others are about challenging ourselves on why and how we use this technique.

Consider how you might utilise the following ideas in your classroom:

- ✓ Reflect on the calling-out behaviour before it happens, considering what motivates it in the first place, to figure out ways in which to pre-empt it. Ideally, we need to put strategies in place to make it unlikely that learners will feel the impulse to shout out.
- ✓ For example, if the issue is with learners feeling the need to be heard, ask them to turn to a talk partner and talk about their ideas, before choosing someone to share with the whole class.
- ✓ If the issue is more around a struggle with impulse control, ask everyone to call out their answer simultaneously, give a non-verbal gesture to supply their answer – such as thumbs up, level or down to indicate yes/maybe/no – or write their response on a mini whiteboard.
- ✓ Consider the *reason* for using a Q&A and what you want to achieve with it. If it is about checking for understanding, there are lots of ways in which to do this that do not involve individuals giving answers to questions in a whole-class scenario. If it is about encouraging your learners to listen to other people's ideas and views, this can also usefully be done in a small group rather than a whole-class format.
- ✓ Choose a random system for getting answers from your class, such as the classic 'lollipop sticks in a pot', where the learners write their names on a stick and these are then drawn out to indicate who should answer. When using random questioning strategies, take care that learners have a chance to prepare an answer (i.e. by using 'talk partners' or similar) and avoid putting nervous learners on the spot.
- ✓ Where we do want to use whole-class Q&A, a useful approach is to give learners a way in which to manage the impulse to call out. This can be done both with individuals and also with a whole class. For instance, as a whole-class strategy, remind learners to 'hit the pause button' before you ask them the question or to take a deep breath before raising a hand to answer. For individuals, find a strategy that offers a positive alternative, such as holding their hand in front of their mouth to remind them not to call out.

Another common problem that teachers identify is children and young people asking what we might call 'pointless' questions. These are the questions that they could probably answer for themselves if they took a moment to think things through. In some ways, these 'pointless' questions seem to be more about learners needing a sense of support and comfort from their teacher, rather than always genuinely wanting an answer. A very useful technique for handling this situation is to approach it as a learning opportunity and to work through the possibilities together with the class.

- ✓ Generate a list of questions together that children or young people might need or want to ask the teacher during a lesson.
- ✓ Now ask the learners to think metacognitively about the questions, to figure out when these questions might or might not be appropriate and when it might be possible to answer them for themselves.
- ✓ Work with the class to put the questions into different categories – for instance, 'solve it myself'/'ask a peer for help'/'ask my teacher'. This helps learners to think through which questions are valid ones to ask the teacher and which could be easily solved in other ways.

This approach is similar to the 'three before me' strategy, where there is a class poster listing lots of things that a learner could potentially try before coming to their teacher for help, such as 'look it up', 'ask a friend' and so on.

Chapter 6
Building Focus and Attentional Control

> In this chapter, we will:
>
> ✓ Explore how attentional control develops over time.
> ✓ Learn about how our brains filter out superfluous sensory information.
> ✓ Explore the concept of attentional control and how we move our attention around.
> ✓ Examine the role of different types of distractions and what we can do about them.
> ✓ Consider the classroom environment and how to manage distractions for our learners.
> ✓ Develop strategies to support learners in directing and maintaining their attention.

In evolutionary terms, our survival as a species has depended on us being able to extract the most relevant signals from those that surround us – to use our senses to pay attention to the 'right things'. In the distant past, this skill would have helped us to spot an approaching threat in the environment or to smell when food had gone off and was not safe to eat, and we still utilise these skills today. The world is filled with sensory information, and if our brains fully paid attention to everything that is around us, we would find it impossible to cope. Fortunately, we can pay attention to specific parts of this sensory information, selectively filtering out the information that we do not need. This is why, when we are focused strongly on one input (for instance, reading a gripping novel on the train journey home), our brains can filter out extraneous information so that we do not notice anything else (for example, the noise of people chatting on the train around us). Attentional control – what we might also call concentration or focus – is the capacity to choose what to pay attention to and what to ignore.

Clearly, one of the key factors supporting effective learning is the way in which we use and focus our attention and the ways in which our teachers encourage and help us to concentrate in class. If our goal is to learn, we need to pay attention to the right things at the right times, and think hard about them. In a classroom situation, this might be about paying attention to what a teacher is saying, listening to a peer, looking at the board to follow what the teacher is writing, watching an experiment to see what happens, filtering out distractions so that we can concentrate on a task and so on. Indeed, it could be argued that 'learning to learn' is about learning how to focus and move our attention around, so that we are able to think hard about what we want to learn and remember.

Any learners who struggle with sensory processing are likely to find it much harder to focus and pay attention than their peers or to suffer from overload because too much information is getting through. When we think about conditions such as ADHD, we can see that the difficulty with the skill of 'paying attention' is specified in the name given to the condition. It is important to remember that the teaching environment can be a key source of distractions. Often, supporting attentional control is about making adaptations to the environment, as well as about incorporating practical strategies to build focus and concentration. Sometimes – perhaps quite frequently – the sensory inputs distracting our learners are outside of our control. It is well-known just how much havoc a windy day can cause in classrooms (particularly when combined with a scattering of snow or an important football match on the weekend).

The development of attentional control

Attentional control is primarily mediated by the frontal areas of the brain, including the anterior cingulate cortex. It is closely linked to other executive functions, such as working memory. This set of skills develops over the course of childhood. While babies struggle to remove their attention from something that 'captures' it, children's frontal lobes progressively mature as they develop, and they gradually become better at moving their attention around and concentrating on a specific goal. The process of filtering out potential distractions appears to start in the prefrontal cortex, a part of the brain that is vital for complex behaviours such as planning and making decisions. It seems that we can inhibit some of our sensory reactions while putting more of our focus on others.

Babies are born with some but not all of their senses fully developed, and their senses play a key part in how they start to make sense of their world. The first sense to develop is smell, and the receptors for this begin to develop in the womb; babies are born with a complete sense of smell and are calmed by the scent of their mother. A baby's sense of touch is also fully developed when they are born, although this develops further as they experience different textures and objects and build motor skills. The sense of taste is also in place from about 17 weeks of gestation. Although a baby's hearing does develop during pregnancy, to the extent that babies can recognise their mother's voice, this sense continues to develop after birth, allowing children to develop their language skills. Sight is one of the last senses to develop and it is not yet fully developed at birth. A baby's vision is fuzzy when they are born and they can only see things close up.

Babies and young children build their understanding of their world through their sensory responses to it – at this stage, lots of diverse sensory information is coming in, which helps their brains to develop. Although sensory information might appear to be less important in a school context, particularly as learners get older, in fact, sensory processing issues can be a key factor in SEND and in difficulties with self-regulation. As educators, we need to be aware of the sensory environment within our classrooms and its potential impact on regulation. We should also keep a lookout for sensory delays or impairments – for instance, glue ear or poor eyesight – which can have significant negative impacts on learning. Where learners appear to struggle with attentional control, checking that their sensory processing has developed as expected is a very useful first port of call.

The mechanism of 'selective attention' allows us to start to process what is relevant to us and inhibit what is not. Once a child can regulate and direct their attention, this allows them to stop responding mainly to their immediate environment and to start putting their attention on the things that will help them to learn. However, we are still naturally prone to having our attention drawn towards novel events in our environment that might prove to be important to us. A loud noise will 'startle' us and instantly draw our attention; bright colours pull our attention and focus. We can see evidence of evolutionary adaptation in the 'warning signs' that some creatures give us, via their colouring, to grab our attention: the colours displayed by a wasp indicating that it might sting or by a poison dart frog telling us not to eat it. Because our attention is affected by information coming into our brains from multiple senses, it is interesting to consider the range of ways in which we process information from our different senses and how different sensory inputs in a classroom will feed into this.

There are essentially two types of attention, and it is useful for teachers to consider the effects of both types within a classroom situation:

- ✓ **voluntary attention**, where learners choose to perform a task by selecting what is relevant and filtering out any background distractions or irrelevant information
- ✓ **involuntary attention**, where unexpected stimuli in the environment lead to distractions (this second one is well known to teachers as an unwelcome distraction from learning).

In early childhood, parents and carers can support children in the process of learning what it is useful to pay attention to within the environment, and teachers can support this process to continue once learners are at school. A parent might talk about the sounds that they hear in the world around them, to help their child understand and 'tune into' important noises and what they mean – the sound of a dog barking in the distance, a bird singing, a plane passing or the sound of the doorbell indicating that 'a visitor' has arrived. Being able to identify and pay attention to different sounds supports areas of learning, such as developing language and building early reading skills. By encouraging our learners to 'tune into' themselves and their environment, we can help them to build focus and attentional control and make sense of their world.

Where learners have sensory processing difficulties, this can have a direct impact on their ability to self-regulate. Because their brains are not filtering out some of the sensory distractions in the world around them, this leaves them much less space to make the rational decisions required to manage their behaviours. For learners with autism, this can lead to sensory overload and what we sometimes refer to as 'meltdowns' or episodes of total dysregulation. These learners may attempt to mask the autistic behaviours, such as stimming, that help them to cope with sensory overload in the classroom, which can mean that we do not see the full issues in a school context. Masking can, however, lead to exhaustion or other difficulties once the learners get home.

We can also use our attentional control to support our emotional self-regulation; we can purposefully distract ourselves from something that is causing a feeling of anxiety. For instance, if we feel nervous about giving a speech, we might try to stop ourselves from worrying by thinking about something else. This effect seems to work in a similar way to the self-distancing described in the previous chapter, which is so helpful for impulse control. We can deliberately move our attention away from something that is troubling or upsetting to us. It is interesting to note that children who are bilingual do better on tasks that require shifting their attention from one thing to another. It seems likely that switching between languages helps these children to learn to think flexibly and to choose how to direct their attention.

Joint attention

Over time, as children develop, they gradually learn to coordinate their attention with others towards a common focus. This forms a key part of social communication because when we share attention, we are referring to the same objects. This helps us develop a shared language, start understanding what other people are thinking and even coordinate our actions. Sports, such as football, are a great example of this, where all the players are focused on 'the ball' and they coordinate their attention to try to get it in the net. Play is a very useful medium for building joint attention, particularly where the children have a common goal in mind – for instance, building a den or planning and playing a game.

Developmentally, the ability to focus our attention on a shared object of interest is usually in place between around nine and 18 months. Research has shown that levels of joint attention in early childhood can predict future social competence, as well as reinforce emotional self-regulation and other key executive functions (Battich et al., 2020). In an educational context, the ability to pay joint attention is hugely important. It is often the case in a classroom that we want to direct our learners' attention to a specific thing, whether this is some writing on the board or a learning resource that we need to discuss with them. When our learners can manage the competing demands on their attention and direct their attention to the right thing at the right time, this inevitably has a positive impact on their learning outcomes.

Joint attention can involve multisensory responses, as well as the more usual visual cues. When we observe someone touching something or someone, this activates similar neural circuits in our brains to those that are involved in the execution of those actions. Multisensory strategies are powerful in building joint attention – for instance, pointing to a toy and simultaneously tapping it so that the child turns their attention towards it. The 'Attention Autism' intervention, developed by speech and language therapist Gina Davies (www.ginadavies.co.uk), is designed to work on aspects such as awareness of others, attention, listening, switching attention and turn-taking. Originally designed to support children with autism, we use this approach in our setting with all our children, and we find it very helpful for supporting attentional control and language development. The intervention involves interesting activities that encourage children to take turns and pay joint attention to their peers, which the teacher supports children to complete. An adult leads the activities, but these are very much focused on being engaging, interesting and fun for the children. They combine multisensory activities, such as blowing bubbles or blowing up a balloon, along with accompanying songs.

Concentration and distractions

Being able to maintain their focus and concentration supports understanding, which, in turn, boosts learners' self-confidence and self-esteem. There are links between visual attention span and reading performance, with poor attention span leading to difficulties with reading. Text comprehension obviously requires us to be able to focus in order to make sense of what we are reading. Distractibility changes with age, as we become more able to choose to give our attention to something. With the maturing of the brain, our attention spans gradually increase, although they only reach full maturity in our mid-twenties. Concentration, attention and distractibility are also influenced by our motivations and our environment. When we are interested in something, we tend to be able to focus our attention more fully on it and for longer. When our environment is overly stimulating, this is likely to lead to additional distractions. In addition, diet and sleep patterns can have a powerful influence on how distractible we are, and consequently, how effective we are at maintaining our concentration.

The sensory information coming at our learners while they are in school must feel overwhelming to some. Our sensory responses to the smells, sights and sounds of school can become strongly embedded as memories. Smell offers one of the longest persisting memories – I can still conjure up the smell of my primary school canteen, 50 years after I last stood in it, particularly because it made me feel nauseous and because I associate the smell with being forced to eat foods that I hated. For some learners in our classrooms, the distractions going on for them might well be internal and not linked to the school environment at all. For example, they feel hungry because they did not have any breakfast or upset about something that is going on at home.

It is obviously very important for educators to be aware of children's varying concentration spans because once we go beyond a certain point in asking them to focus, their concentration naturally drops off. At this point, they stop taking in and processing the information that we are giving them and they are likely to try to distract themselves, most likely with inappropriate behaviours. Anyone who has ever tried to talk to a group of young children for a long period will recognise the issue, as they start to wriggle and look – or even walk – away. Similarly, even as adults we are prone to losing our attentional control and focus – for instance, in a CPD session. The answer to a loss of concentration is usually around a change of approach rather than just plugging on regardless. This might mean taking a quick break, standing up for a quick movement activity or participating in something interactive, such as discussing ideas with a group.

A very useful rule of thumb that someone told me about years ago in relation to concentration is 'their age, plus two' for how long children can concentrate on a single thing. In other words, with a five-year-old, you have roughly seven minutes of attentional control on a single task before you need to swap to something else or incorporate a quick physical or mental break. With a 15-year-old, you have roughly 17 minutes in which they can maintain full focus before it is useful to give them some kind of refresher break. Clearly, as learners age, they are expected to concentrate for longer and longer periods, with end-of-school exams requiring long periods of intense concentration. It is obviously important for teachers of older learners to practise this with their classes, so that they build up their stamina when focusing. However, day to day in a classroom, and indeed for revision, it is more effective for learning if children and young people work in shorter chunks.

Sometimes distractions in the classroom will occur as part of the lesson – for instance, when something goes completely wrong or even as part of the approach to teaching and learning, where an exciting resource or idea is presented. Many teachers will have experienced that moment when you say or do something that the learners find amusing or exciting, and the class immediately becomes highly distractible and it is tricky to get them to return their focus. I find myself doing this when I work with adults as well – a kind of 'self-sabotage'. It may be the case that these accidental distractions are useful for the group to let off steam. When we are thinking about self-regulation, we should remember not to take everything too seriously and to be realistic in our expectations of what young people can or should achieve.

Indeed, when we are thinking about the importance of paying attention, it is useful to remember that sitting and staring off into the distance (i.e. daydreaming) can be a method for heightening creativity and distilling or making sense of our ideas. Interestingly, research (Sun et al., 2022) demonstrates both positive and negative learning outcomes associated with daydreaming. While we might not want a class full of learners to be daydreaming simultaneously, especially if a member of the senior leadership team has dropped in, there should certainly be space in our thinking for exploring the benefits of switching off our attention, as well as switching it on.

SLANT and attentional control

It may be helpful to consider the technique of 'SLANT' (Lemov, 2023) in the context of attentional control and getting the attention of the class, particularly because it has become increasingly popular in UK schools in recent years. It is claimed that the acronym stands for a range of things, usually along the lines of 'sit up, listen, ask and answer questions, nod your head and track the speaker'. Interestingly, where the technique is used in UK schools, the 'N' in the acronym seems to have been reinterpreted (for instance, as 'never interrupt'), perhaps to acknowledge that asking learners to nod on command feels highly awkward in this context. The claims made for the technique include the idea that you put the habits in place first to encourage attention, and that these habits then become ingrained.

However, critics have raised the point that it seems important to consider questions around authenticity and effective communication, as discussed in Chapter 3. How does the teacher *know* that the learners are paying attention and thinking hard about what is being said, rather than just positioning their bodies in the way that is demanded? Where aspects such as eye contact and body language are insisted on by the teacher, valuable feedback based on more naturalistic forms of non-verbal communication may get overlooked. The answer to these questions seems to be to use what is referred to as 'cold calling', i.e. to insist that learners listen by the use of random questioning. It is worth considering how learners with high levels of anxiety might feel about this technique being used.

Commentators, especially those with expertise in special needs, have also questioned the effect of this technique on learners with ADHD and other types of SEND (Hawker, 2021). In particular, the demand to make eye contact can be problematic for learners with autism because they can struggle with this and may tend to look at the details of the teacher's eyes, rather than thinking about what is being said. An insistence on sitting up straight may be tricky for learners with physical difficulties, such as weak proprioception. Another useful question to ask is about the role of agency and learner choice – so crucial in the development of self-regulation. The balance between teacher direction and learner agency is vital to consider if we want to develop intrinsic motivation to self-regulate – the research shows that too much structure can be as problematic as too little.

Practical strategies for the classroom

As with all aspects of self-regulation, one of the key strategies that we need to invoke to help us build focus and concentration is to encourage our learners to think about managing themselves and building their ability to pay attention – in other words, to take steps to get learners to think metacognitively about how their brains and their thinking work. It is also useful to encourage them to reflect on the kinds of things that cause them to feel distracted, whether this is peers, the weather or something specific in the environment. They can then figure out the best methods for avoiding those issues on a personal level with your support. You might ask:

- ✓ What kinds of things disrupt or distract you from learning?
- ✓ Is this the same as or different to the things that distract your peers?
- ✓ What could you do to help yourself to ignore the distractions?
- ✓ How can you help your peers to avoid getting distracted?
- ✓ Which of your senses is most likely to cause a distraction: sight, hearing, touch, taste or smell?
- ✓ What is the best kind of environment for you in terms of learning?
- ✓ Which sensory inputs are most likely to support your concentration?
- ✓ How do you know when you need a break from focusing and paying attention?
- ✓ What kind of break works best to refresh you?

It is also useful to talk to your learners about the kinds of useful strategies that they can use when they do find themselves losing focus or becoming distracted, particularly outside of the school environment. For example, they might:

- ✓ take a short walk or do something physical to reboot their thinking
- ✓ talk things through with a friend – for instance, if they are distracted by a worry or concern
- ✓ have a quick laugh (or cry) about the distraction before settling on a task
- ✓ use their imagination to take themselves to a 'happy place' and block out the distraction.

A useful technique to share with learners involves analysing the situation rationally to reframe the distraction for the future. For example, if they are nervous about wasps because they worry that they might get stung, they could consider the likelihood of getting stung and whether this is higher or lower if they panic and flap at the insect.

Attention and the teacher

Another useful factor to consider is where *you* put your attention as the teacher and how this might impact what happens in terms of attention, focus and learning in your lessons. We have a natural tendency as educators for our attention to be drawn to those learners who are doing the wrong thing. Unfortunately, paying attention to learners who are behaving inappropriately is likely to reinforce the behaviours that we do not want to see. Be aware of this instinctive impulse and train yourself to widen your attention to the whole class, rather than focusing on individuals. Identify at least five positive examples of learner behaviour ('That's great, you're sitting silent and ready to learn, thanks!') before you deal with any examples of the behaviour that you do not want.

Subconsciously, we tend to teach to the side of the classroom that is on our dominant side (i.e. the right side of the room if we are right-handed and the left if we are left-handed). This can mean that learners on the far left or far right sides of the room receive less attention than others, and that one side of the room tends to benefit more from our focus. To help you avoid this issue:

- ✓ Be consciously aware of your impulse to 'teach to the right' if you are right-handed (or vice versa if left-handed) and make a deliberate, conscious attempt to give your attention to the learners on the left-hand side of the room.
- ✓ Aim to build an underlying awareness of how much 'coverage' different individuals in the class have had in terms of your attention, by keeping this thought in your mind and checking in on yourself from time to time.
- ✓ Be conscious of any learners who need a bit more reassurance than others, and do a quick 'check-in' with your eyes to indicate 'I am noticing you' regularly. You can also scaffold this during class tasks, by giving the learner a timer and saying that you will return to check on them when the timer runs out.

- ✓ Move around the space to let the learners know that you are spreading your attention around the room, but also that you are liable to 'pop up' anywhere at any time. This tends to keep the learners on their toes.
- ✓ When thinking about spreading your attention around the room, be conscious of anyone who has a hearing impairment. For these learners, ensure that your body and face are directed towards them when you are speaking, and articulate your mouth and lip movements to help them read what you are saying.
- ✓ Aim for moments of complete stillness, as well as times when you are roaming around. It is easier for your learners to concentrate on important content when you are static. Many teachers have what they call a 'silent spot', where they always or usually stand when they want to address the whole class.
- ✓ Your 'silent spot' can end up becoming an indicator that you are waiting for the attention of the class. Experiment with just going to stand there but without saying anything next time you want the class to return to you, and see what happens.

You can combine physical movement around the room with use of your eyes to indicate 'I am focused on this particular thing at the moment':

- ✓ Scan the room without letting your eyes alight on any individual learners, to show that you are 'scanning for information'. This is particularly useful when you have set a task because it will tell you whether everyone has understood, whether they have got straight down to work, whether they are focused or distracted and so on. When I am training teachers, I refer to this as 'CCTV' because we are basically 'scanning the area for trouble'.
- ✓ Zoom your eyes and your attention in on one learner when they are answering a question or giving an idea to the class, almost like a spotlight. Move towards them slightly to show that you are interested in what they are saying. I call this a 'zoom lens' in my CPD sessions.
- ✓ You can also raise your eyes to the ceiling to indicate that you have deliberately removed your attention from the class and that you are waiting for them to fall silent before you return your gaze to them. This is surprisingly effective if they are used to you always looking them in the eyes, and especially if combined with the use of a 'silent spot'.

Getting the attention of the class

As well as wanting our learners to *pay* attention, we also need them to *give* us their complete attention at the right moments during a lesson. This might be when we need to directly teach them something, when we want to clarify a point while they are working on an activity, when we need to give them instructions and so on – in other words, at multiple points during a typical school day. There are as many ways of getting a class's attention as there are teachers, and I have heard numerous creative solutions and interesting ideas over the years. These fall into a variety of categories, as listed below, with a few examples of each one:

- ✓ a sound, such as a handbell, a singing bowl or a xylophone
- ✓ a visual indicator, such as raising an arm in the air or turning off the lights
- ✓ a physical activity, such as taking your pulse or doing a quick game of 'Teacher says' (like 'Simon says' but to return the learners to you)
- ✓ a spoken choral exchange, also called 'call and respond', such as teacher: '1, 2, 3, eyes on me'; learners: '1, 2, eyes on you'
- ✓ a movement, such as the 'spirit fingers' that one teacher shared with me – basically wiggling your fingers in the air in a gathering motion, as though to 'draw' the class towards you
- ✓ a 'non-signal', such as standing on a silent spot or falling silent and folding your arms.

Something that I have observed over the years is that 'silent signals' tend to run out of steam after you have been using them for a while. When you notice that the class are slower in responding to the attention signal that you are giving them, this is usually a clue that it is time to change it up and try something new.

Thinking about the environment

We tend to approach classroom practice by thinking about our techniques as teachers, but in addition to developing these skills, we can also support learners to better focus in our classrooms by thinking about the impact of the wider environment. Consider what aspects of the environment might prove distracting for your learners and how you might manage or minimise these distractions to help them focus. This is not always possible; some elements of the teaching environment are outside of our direct control. For instance, if your school is near a busy road, there will inevitably be noise pollution, or if your windows look out over the front of the building, your learners may be distracted by deliveries and visitors to the school. However, with a bit of lateral thinking, there is often something that can be done about the environment to improve the potential for learners to focus and pay attention.

- ✓ Learn to see the environment and the space from the learners' perspective to help identify distractions and find strategies to deal with them. It is very useful indeed to go and sit in several different spots in your classroom when the learners are not there, to see what the room and the environment look and feel like from their perspective.

- ✓ Be realistic about what might distract your learners – if something would draw *your* attention, then do not expect your learners to be able to resist. Sometimes it is better to acknowledge the distraction and let your learners process it than to always demand complete attention.
- ✓ Remember that your learners will be interacting with their environment using all their senses. We tend to think about minimising distractions as meaning cutting visual clutter, but clearly, our attention is drawn by other sensory responses.
- ✓ While visual inputs might be more distracting to some learners, auditory ones could be far more troubling to others, so take a moment to close your eyes and pick up on any auditory distractions. (A good example of how people respond differently to a variety of sensory inputs is to consider whether you prefer to work with or without background music or radio. For some people (me), silence is essential to be able to work, particularly when I am writing; for other people (my partner), music is essential to be able to work.)
- ✓ Remember that minimising distractions is categorically *not* about stripping out all the visual information from a classroom because that would strip out all the challenge and it is challenge that supports learning.
- ✓ Think instead about where you place visual information and keep multiple sources of visual information separate from one another.
- ✓ Consider how you can get rid of extraneous visual clutter – for instance, posters that are not referred to or displays that are overly 'busy'.
- ✓ Find ways in which to incorporate focus exercises and to manage obvious distractions – for example, by limiting the number of items on the learners' desks.

Of course, we do not need to make our learners feel like school is the equivalent of a monastery, where they are only allowed to focus on 'the learning', entirely separate from the wider environment – education is about much more than that. Although if we strip the walls and minimise visible clutter it might, in theory, make it 'easier' to concentrate and focus the class on exactly what the teacher wants them to process and remember, our learners need to learn how to manage real-world environments. In life, they will constantly encounter situations where it is quite tricky to focus and maintain their attention, and yet they will still need to do so. We do not do learners any favours by creating a completely artificial environment because this means that they do not get to practise managing distractions.

Managing visuals

It is very helpful to sit where the learners sit in your room, to look at the front of the room where you usually stand and ask yourself: What happens if there are too many visuals in the area around my interactive whiteboard? Often, this is the place where primary teachers will stick up charts, references, timelines, days of the week, behaviour charters and various other useful bits of information, as a handy reference resource. In secondary classrooms, this space can be filled up with displays of subject-specific vocabulary, terminology, charts, tables and other subject-based information. However, it is useful to question ourselves about this.

Some useful questions to consider include:

- ✓ What will the learners see when they are looking at me as I teach?
- ✓ Where should I stand to make it easiest for the learners to focus on what I am saying? (Consider the lighting conditions when you do this – being backlit by a window can make it harder for them to see.)
- ✓ When I ask my learners to 'look at the board', what is likely to draw their attention?
- ✓ Can I keep the area directly around my interactive whiteboard clear of extraneous information?
- ✓ Could I locate additional information (e.g. days of the week, subject vocabulary, etc.) on the side or back walls instead?

As well as thinking about the potential for distractions from visual 'clutter', consider other visual aspects of your classroom too, such as:

- ✓ Although you may not be able to do much about it, it is useful to consider the role of lighting in supporting attention and focus for your learners. Children with SEND can be sensitive to the flickering that happens with strip lights (a very common feature in many schools).
- ✓ Consider switching artificial lights off on a bright day, or ask the school to change from strip lights to alternative methods for lighting classrooms.
- ✓ Think about the colours that you choose – for instance, for displays – remembering that colour affects mood. Consider the impact of warm and cold colours on attention – warm, bright colours can help to energise, while cooler, pastel shades will tend to calm.
- ✓ Remember that visuals can be a positive for attention as well as potentially a distraction. For example, visual reminders such as cards, timers, objects, etc. are great to help scaffold understanding.
- ✓ Resources offer a way in which to 'grab' a class's attention and to make the learning concrete. When we use multisensory concrete visuals, these combine lots of interest to draw the children's attention, so it is always a balance between too much and too little.

Managing auditory inputs

Classrooms are obviously extremely auditory places – the teacher talks, the learners answer, the chairs scrape. Occasionally, a wonderful silence falls on the room, only to be broken by the distracting noise of a learner doing something inappropriate. Managing noise levels, particularly when learners are talking, will help you to support all of them, but particularly anyone who experiences sensory overload. Model what 'quiet' looks like by managing your own volume levels so that the learners get used to having to listen hard (but not too hard) so that they can hear what you are saying. Model what listening and being silent look like too. Bear in mind that some younger learners may have glue ear or a hearing impairment, perhaps undiagnosed, so be on the lookout for those who do not seem to be properly responsive to noise or who are having speech and language difficulties that might indicate issues with their hearing.

Ask yourself what other sensory inputs learners are experiencing and how you might adapt or minimise the potential of these to distract. For instance, the sound of a data projector whirring might be distracting for some learners, so it could be that this can be switched off when it is not in use. If there is a great deal of traffic noise coming in from outside, a longer-term solution could involve planting hedges to baffle the sound and to reduce wind speed. Think about the impact of noise *between* classrooms and teaching spaces in your school. Where one class is particularly noisy, this can filter into the room next door. At the same time, the 'buzz' of a school full of active learners will inevitably involve some higher levels of noise from time to time, and it is important that we help our learners to handle this situation too.

When managing auditory inputs, again we should think about learner agency. We need to encourage our learners to take control of this aspect of their classroom experience. It helps to be explicit about different levels of noise and when each level is appropriate – for instance, practising with the class to find an acceptable level for different activities. Teachers often divide this into categories something like this:

- ✓ silent zone
- ✓ partner voice
- ✓ classroom voice
- ✓ playground voice
- ✓ emergency voice.

You can also use concrete resources to indicate noise levels – for example, a 'noise-o-meter' (bought or homemade for a touch of fun).

'Quiet critters' are a great example for primary teachers of how the imagination can be combined with concrete resources and creative strategies to support attentional control (and elicit the development of empathy). These are small 'creatures' that you introduce to the class as 'quiet critters', and obviously quiet critters require low noise levels. The imaginative empathy that the learners will hopefully develop towards the critters will help them build their impulse control around noise levels, and in turn, support an environment that promotes attentional control. Here is a description of how 'quiet critters' work:

- ✓ Create a selection of quiet critters using coloured pom-poms with stuck-on googly eyes. You can also use the stick-on pom-pom creatures sometimes given away as a marketing tool.
- ✓ Place your critters in a plastic fish tank and create a 'habitat' for them by using sticks, pebbles or other resources of your choice.
- ✓ Cover the fish tank with a cloth and bring it into your classroom to show the learners, explaining that there are 'quiet critters' inside and that they are very scared of noise.
- ✓ Once the children have got over their initial excitement, encourage them to control the noise levels so that you can show them the critters. Remind them that if the noise levels go up, they will scare the critters and you will need to cover them up again.
- ✓ Show the tank of critters to the children and put it in a prominent place in your classroom. Explain that if a child is working super-sensibly and quietly, one of the critters might even feel brave enough to come out of the tank and sit beside them.

You could involve the children in deciding whether the class is quiet enough for the critters to come out and whom they might like to sit beside. Giving the learners the agency to get involved in the decision-making process helps them to understand how they can regulate and manage their own behaviours.

At secondary classroom level, a decibel meter can be useful for identifying when the noise is getting too much. Alternatively, apps such as 'Too Noisy' offer ways in which to manage noise, using visual and auditory signals. Again, consider handing over responsibility for managing noise levels to the learners.

Strategies for directing and maintaining attention

When children try to process a lot of information at once, this can overload their working memory and make it harder for them to maintain attention on what they are supposed to be doing – for instance, when they are following a series of instructions. Teachers can scaffold the retention and processing of the information for them, and in doing so support their attentional control. Many of the strategies for doing this are just basic good teaching practice.

For instance:

- ✓ using visuals and symbols to support spoken or written instructions
- ✓ chunking instructions up so that you only give a few at a time
- ✓ using repetition to ensure that something is understood
- ✓ reframing and rephrasing information to ensure that the vocabulary is clear for everyone
- ✓ asking for an example to check for understanding
- ✓ being explicit about what is to be done in each step
- ✓ creating a mnemonic for learners to use to recall the information
- ✓ offering a checklist of actions to complete.

We can also use narratives and songs to support recall, processing and attentional control. For example, our preschool children sing a song about crossing the road when we are about to cross the road on our daily walk. This reminds them to follow each of the steps in turn, and the song makes it easier for them to recall and remember the actions that they need to take. In an environment with lots of sensory information, such as being outdoors, the song gives them something specific on which to focus.

A key time when learners are likely to be distracted is just after a break. They will often come back into the classroom with their minds on all the things that just happened in the playground, such as falling out with a friend, scraping a knee or not getting a turn in a game. Instead of expecting children and young people to instantly be able to redirect their attention from these emotional aspects of the school day and onto subject learning, it is useful to incorporate chances to offload and clear their minds. There are various ways in which you can do this:

- ✓ A 'minute to moan' can usefully channel learners' focus into offloading anything that happened during a break that is worrying them. Explain to the class that you want them to turn to talk to a partner and that they now have a 'minute to moan', i.e. to offload all the things that are bothering them. Use a timer to increase focus and to show that this is limited to one minute.
- ✓ Set up a postbox and offer a stack of postcards with some pens or pencils. Explain to the learners that if they are worried about something that happened prior to the lesson, they should write a note on a card and post it in the box. You will then chat with them about it at an appropriate moment.

A stream of consciousness exercise is also very useful for clearing the learners' minds, particularly where a lesson is going to involve substantial amounts of writing:

- ✓ Explain to the learners that you are going to ask them to write for around two minutes and that there are some 'rules' that they should follow.
- ✓ When you say 'go', they should begin to write and they should not stop writing until you say 'stop'.
- ✓ If they get stuck, they should write the same word over and over again until they get unstuck.
- ✓ The idea is to write down anything that comes into their minds, without worrying about whether it makes sense. They are aiming to 'cut out' the 'internal critic' that comments on what they are doing and just get their thoughts down on the page.
- ✓ They do not need to worry about punctuation, spelling, grammar or anything technical because no one is going to check this. It is literally a piece of writing to clear the mind rather than something written to make sense.
- ✓ At the end of the activity, it can work well to give your learners permission to throw their stream of consciousness away.
- ✓ Explain to the class that this is similar to the way in which you want them to throw away any negative thoughts from break as they enter the lesson because these might interfere with their learning.

Mindfulness and attentional control

Mindfulness and meditation activities are essentially an exercise in attentional control – we are encouraged to focus our attention on a specific part of the body, on visualising a specific thing or on stilling our thoughts. There has recently been a lot of interest in mindfulness from neuroscientists and other researchers (e.g. Sørensen et al., 2018). Various studies suggest that mindfulness can improve overall wellbeing, support attentional control and help people to act with more autonomy when pursuing intrinsic motivations. These activities can help beyond the classroom as well, with potential impacts on areas as diverse as mental health and job satisfaction levels.

Mindfulness activities typically include a series of facets, as described in questionnaires such as the 'Five Facets Mindfulness Questionnaire' (Baer et al., 2006). These are:

- ✓ **observing** – noticing inner reactions, sensations and experiences
- ✓ **non-judging** – making these observations without judgement
- ✓ **describing** – putting inner experiences of perceptions, thoughts, feelings, etc. into words
- ✓ **non-reactive** – avoiding a reaction to inner experiences
- ✓ **acting with awareness** – the voluntary focus of attention.

When using mindfulness activities with children and young people, this might be incorporated as part of your daily provision (for instance, a short meditation session after lunch) or as a starter activity for lessons. Repetitive activities, such as colouring, can act as a 'working meditation', where the repetitive nature of the activity stills the mind. The internet is full of suggestions for different types of mindfulness activities, underlining the recent popularity of this technique, particularly given levels of concern around young people's mental health and wellbeing.

Chapter 7
Developing Emotional Self-Regulation

In this chapter, we will:

- ✓ Think about what we mean when we talk about 'emotions' and 'feelings'.
- ✓ Consider the role that interoception plays in becoming aware of our emotional state.
- ✓ Explore ways for teachers to help learners to become more aware of their emotions.
- ✓ Consider how educators can help themselves to stay on an even keel emotionally.
- ✓ Examine strategies for supporting learners to manage emotions in the classroom.
- ✓ Look at strategies to help young people to calm themselves when they become dysregulated.

Of all the areas of the subject of self-regulation that have caught the imagination of educators, it is emotional self-regulation that is probably central. You have most likely come across various approaches to support emotional regulation, such as 'zones of regulation' or 'emotions coaching'. Teachers are clearly aware that children and young people bring their emotions to the classroom, and that these emotions can either help or hinder the process of learning. We do not simply 'deliver' curriculum content; we build a relationship within which children and young people feel safe and supported to learn. We influence the mood and attitudes of our learners, through the emotions that we demonstrate around behaviour, learning and teaching, and they, in turn, influence us through their emotional reactions to what happens in school.

When we teach children about emotional self-regulation, we help them understand how to monitor their physiological state of arousal, and in turn, manage their emotional state. As well as helping them to manage feelings and emotions, the same physiological responses also help learners to monitor and manage other external factors that might impact learning – for instance, learning how they can know when their body is telling them they are hungry, learning that this might have an impact on their ability to learn and learning that therefore they should have something to eat. The school and classroom environment elicit both positive and negative emotions in learners and in us, their teachers. When we can support learners to stay on an 'even keel', this allows them to stay in tune with what they are learning at school. In addition, as educators, we must manage our *own* emotions – tricky in some situations, particularly when we are under pressure, defensive or stressed.

This chapter looks at how teachers can support learners to become more aware of their emotions and help them understand why certain emotions arise and how they can best be managed. It also explores how we can identify and respond to emotions in other people – an important aspect of emotional self-regulation that feeds into how we learn empathy (see Chapter 8, page 117). This chapter also explores the strategies that we can use as teachers to ensure that our own emotions help to create a positive classroom climate. It is important to remember that the emphasis should not be on eliminating emotional reactions. Emotions give us important feedback about ourselves and our environment, and expressing them supports mental health and wellbeing. When considering emotional self-regulation, our emphasis should be on acknowledging emotions, and then confidently handling them.

The development of emotional regulation

As with the other areas of self-regulation explored in this book, emotional regulation first develops within the relationship between a child and their caregivers from birth. In early infancy, babies need their carers to be responsive to their needs, particularly when they are feeling distress. When the baby's needs are met consistently and promptly, they start to trust that those around them will respond to them sensitively when they are in need. The child and their caregivers participate in 'serve and return' interactions (see page 31), which, in turn, help to build the architecture of the child's brain.

The term 'behavioural synchrony' describes the ways in which parents and carers resonate with and adapt to their children's verbal and non-verbal communications – in other words, how they respond to and 'mirror' the child's communications. Where synchrony develops between carers and their children, this supports the development of emotional regulation and the associated skill of empathy. Emotionally attuned parenting involves coordinating the various social signals that pass between them and their child, including gaze, voice, effect and touch. The parent and child form a bond in which this synchrony is experienced and encoded in the child's brain. This, in turn, creates a pattern for the child in later life, when they come across other people who exhibit feelings of distress, upset and so on.

The sympathetic and parasympathetic nervous systems make up the autonomic nervous system, and these develop in the context of these emotionally attuned interactions with caregivers (Köhler-Dauner et al., 2022). The sympathetic nervous system controls our 'fight or flight' responses, preparing us for sudden physical activity. The parasympathetic nervous system regulates our 'rest and digest' functions, when we are not in a situation where we might perceive a threat. The vagus nerve forms an integral part of the autonomic nervous system, and this, in turn, links to the development of interoception (see page 100). Where caregiving is sensitive and responsive, this has been shown to support the organisation of these response systems, which, in turn, can help children to self-regulate more effectively. In other words, where parents or carers are responsive, children know that they are going to be supported and their bodies react to that information. Conversely, it is important to remember that exposure to stress, adversity or maternal depression can lead to issues with the development of the autonomic nervous system and, in turn, with self-regulation.

With the support and care of the adults around them, children learn that they can navigate situations that are beyond their current developmental capabilities and they also become better able to self-regulate in the future. They use these positive experiences of caring to learn how to soothe themselves – self-soothing is the starting point for learning to manage our emotions. In other words, adults co-regulate with the child until they can start to regulate for themselves. Adults model for children how it is possible to pause between experiencing difficult feelings and reacting to them. This supports children to learn how to take time to think and plan when they experience intense emotions. When children experience a range of social situations and learn how to cope with them, they build the capacity to regulate their emotions for themselves.

Interestingly, the skill of being able to express some key emotions happens very early on, around the first six months of life. These key emotions are linked to very specific facial expressions, which are the same or very similar across different countries and cultures. These appear to be innate – or biologically determined – and include anger, fear, joy, sadness, disgust and surprise. Researchers have proposed that this is because these expressions are linked to human survival – they are emotions that help us to form social groups, know when something such as food or water might be bad for us, and react to unexpected external stimuli. It is interesting to consider how we feel philosophically about emotions – do we perceive them as either 'good' or 'bad', and how might this influence the way in which we handle them?

The role of interoception in feelings

There is a complex relationship between how the body and mind interact when we experience what we refer to as 'emotions' or 'feelings'. Both physiological and cognitive elements are involved in the process of identifying and naming emotions. Feelings are essentially an embodied response to an external stimulus. The stimulus that elicits emotions can be either real or perceived, and it can be internal or external. For instance, learners might get nervous about an upcoming exam because of both internal and external pressures on them to 'do well'. They might get angry about a perceived slight from a classmate, when in fact they have misunderstood something that was said. We are very much emotional beings and the feelings that we experience help us to understand and cope with the world that we inhabit. Our emotional reactions can be automatic – where we wince, turn away or close our eyes to avoid seeing a particularly scary moment in a movie – or they can be conscious – forcing ourselves to smile in a job interview, even though we are feeling nervous.

The experience that we typically describe using the word 'feelings' is closely linked to interoception. This is sometimes described as our 'eighth sense' and it is the process by which we become aware of and respond to the sensory information that we receive from our organs. This information comes via the vagus nerve, which is the tenth cranial nerve, extending from the brainstem through the neck and thorax and into the abdomen. The 'feelings' that are sent to us by our organs, via this nerve, are translated into what we refer to as 'emotions' or an 'emotional response'. We can sometimes misinterpret or mix up these physiological signals – for example, not realising that our irritation is mainly caused by low blood sugar levels rather than by something that someone has done.

Our bodies can also react to emotions with specific physical symptoms. For instance, we might say that we are feeling anxious when we feel our stomach clenching and our heart racing and we experience a nauseous feeling. We might even need the toilet or be physically sick. The 'feeling of anxiety' is expressed through the way in which our organs react to specific stimuli and the sensory information that is sent to the brain. Similarly, we might say that we are feeling 'angry' when our fists clench, our shoulders tense and our body shakes. Interestingly, many common phrases that we use to describe emotional reactions acknowledge this link between the body and the mind – for example, when we say that someone has 'got under our skin', that we are 'sick to the stomach' or that we 'feel like a bag of nerves'. It can be quite shocking to feel the sudden onset of these sensory inputs.

Interoception has a vital role in our survival because it supports our regulated responses to different sensations, which give us important information to help us stay alive – for instance, sensations of hunger, temperature and pain, which trigger us to find food, warmth or medical care. Sensations related to social integration, such as affection, and those directed towards physical survival, such as fear, anger or aggression, can also be important survival mechanisms. When our body tells us to fight back or run away, what we call our 'emotional state' can help us to survive a physical attack or dangerous encounter. In essence, our body's stress response system is reacting to our environment, to try to help us stay safe and secure. Where our environment feels safe and secure, we are in turn more likely to feel calm, happy and emotionally balanced.

Research has shown that stress and trauma can affect our ability to sense and interpret interoceptive information. In other words, some learners will struggle more than others with sensory processing and understanding what their bodies are trying to tell them about their emotional state. When people respond too much to the stressors that they perceive in the environment, they may become overstimulated or lose emotional control. Many educators will have seen a child go into what we might call 'meltdown', where they are completely dysregulated by an excess of sensory input. Similarly, where people are not responsive enough to the stressors, they may under-respond and disengage or shut down when facing difficulties. Again, many educators will have seen a learner 'blank them' or refuse to engage when a situation becomes too difficult to process.

Emotional regulation and our sense of self

If we hope to be able to regulate our emotions, we first need to build a coherent relationship with our sense of 'self'. We need to become aware of how our body, mind and feelings are communicating with each other in response to the experiences that we are going through. We need to be able to accurately detect and evaluate the various cues in our bodies that relate to our physiological reactions to the events that we are experiencing. We then need to learn how to control and manage our reactions to these events, so that we can feel the emotions but not become overwhelmed by them. This is a tall order, and we should be careful that we do not expect children and young people to be as emotionally aware and literate as adults, especially those children who have faced adverse childhood experiences. It is worth reflecting constantly on our own struggles to handle our emotions, to remind ourselves that it really is OK sometimes not to be able to cope well with the stresses and pressures that we face.

When we are responsive to the interoceptive information that our bodies send us, this allows us to 'get ahead' of our emotional reactions and helps us to manage them, where necessary, to maintain a balanced sense of emotion. Different people experience sensory information in different ways, noticing and holding their 'feelings' in different parts of the body. This is why it is useful to encourage learners to discuss their emotions in detail, and in turn, develop a sense of themselves as separate and unique in the way in which they experience the world. Young children will tend to happily label their emotional states in response to adult questioning, but might not yet be fully tuned into how they can experience and describe their feelings. We need to take care that children do not just tell us what they think we want to hear, but instead encourage them to build a clear sense of themselves and how feelings are experienced for them personally.

When children and young people do not receive enough sensory information, they may feel the need for stronger biofeedback. This can lead to problematic behaviours, such as hitting themselves, making too much noise or banging too hard on a surface. In these situations, the child is trying to increase the volume of the sensory information. They literally want to *feel* more strongly, to build their own sense of themselves in the world. People who have autism can have specific difficulties in matching their external communication of emotion with the 'feelings' that their bodies are telling them about. Their self-perception may not match their external communication of the emotion, and so they might misinterpret what others are feeling or others might 'read' their emotional state incorrectly. To understand more about interoceptive awareness and how this facilitates emotional regulation and a sense of self, read the study by Price and Hooven in the Further Reading section.

Acknowledging and handling emotions

Researchers have explored the differences between learning to acknowledge and handle our emotions – referred to as 'reappraisal' – learning to suppress them – referred to as 'suppression' –and simply learning to accept them (Gross and John, 2003). Where we acknowledge and reappraise our emotions, this is cognitive in nature: we think about and then reframe an emotional situation. For instance, a person might respond to a feeling of low mood by deciding to go for a walk because they know that this will help to boost their mood. This approach is generally considered a positive one because it is flexible and it can be applied to different situations. Evidence suggests that using this approach is associated with lower levels of depression and better wellbeing (Cutuli, 2014). Talking through emotions with our learners and encouraging them to appraise and reframe them is a useful technique to help them think metacognitively about self-regulation.

In contrast, suppression is about experiencing the emotion but inhibiting our responses to it and stopping ourselves from expressing it in our behaviour (for instance, refusing to let ourselves cry when we are upset). This is considered a more negative approach because the emotion persists but it is not acknowledged. It is also less about exploring emotions within a social context, where we might share our feelings with others to help us handle them. Suppression can create a mismatch between what we are feeling and what others perceive us as feeling because we are not showing our emotions externally. This takes a lot of effort and it can create the feeling that we are not being authentic with others. Where people mask their inner feelings, research has shown that they tend to experience fewer positive emotions and have lower self-esteem (Cutuli, 2014). This supports the idea that we should encourage our learners to become emotionally literate, rather than trying to suppress their emotions so that they can 'get on with' learning.

There is also evidence to suggest that some emotional regulation happens automatically, based on our prior experiences and the habits that we have developed over time – for instance, because of negative childhood experiences (Šimić et al., 2021). In these instances, we are not even aware that we are regulating or suppressing our emotions because the regulation is happening on a subconscious level. This is referred to as 'automatic emotion regulation' (Mauss et al., 2007), and it can result in a defensive mechanism – a way of avoiding feelings that are intolerably painful or incredibly hard for us to deal with. We may notice this in a classroom context where a learner seems to shut down and refuse to engage.

Emotions and learning

One of the reasons why it is so important for teachers to help their learners manage their emotions – beyond it being a good thing to do for their wellbeing and psychological health generally – is the impact that our emotions have on our learning. Emotions are closely linked to other self-regulatory skills such as attentional control – we are all likely to have felt difficulty focusing when we are going through an emotional upset. Our emotions also underpin skills such as creative and critical thinking, problem-solving and decision-making – all vital skills for learning. Negative emotions, such as feeling sad, worried or fearful, will clearly impede what a child is able to do in a classroom situation because their mind will be elsewhere. If a learner feels a sense of threat – for instance, from an inability to understand what the teacher is saying or from a poor relationship with a peer in the class – this will clearly limit their learning. The learner's brain and body fight for their survival against the fear of the threat, probably by triggering an angry or defensive response.

Similarly, emotions are linked closely to motivation and, in turn, to our interests, what we enjoy doing and where we feel that we are capable. When we find an inherent joy in learning a specific topic or area of the curriculum and it makes us feel positive emotions, we are more likely to be motivated to continue learning, even if it becomes difficult for us. Research suggests that where we are intrinsically motivated to do something, we are likely to choose more challenging tasks than we might otherwise select (Bandura, 1991). In addition, the more capable we perceive ourselves to be, and the better our self-image, the more likely we are to set higher goals for ourselves and work hard to achieve them. This leads to the need for teachers to consider how they can incorporate learner interests into the classroom and how they can support learners to become more intrinsically motivated.

Issues with emotional regulation

You have probably noticed that some children and young people find it much harder to manage their emotions than others. There may be various potential reasons for this – some environmental, probably about their early childhood experiences, others genetic or linked to being in a disadvantaged home situation at present. Recent research (Henriques, 2019; Yehuda, 2022) has suggested that traumas experienced as young children can actually leave genetic marks on a child, which are, in turn, passed down to the next generation. Some common factors that might cause difficulty in regulating emotionally are discussed below:

- ✓ Issues around secure attachments can mean that a child has not had the experience of their feelings being supported and translated for them by the adults around them. When children have had more experience of fear and anxiety in their bodies, they may not know what to do to calm themselves down.
- ✓ Children with autism can struggle to identify their emotions or, conversely, show very little emotional reaction at all. This can lead to confusion and overwhelm when the child does experience a strong emotion because they have little experience of handling it or understanding it.
- ✓ Learners who have ADHD can very quickly get frustrated by things that others might find mildly irritating. They will sometimes worry excessively about minor things, appear overly sensitive or feel an urgency to do something and act on impulse.

When children and young people experience overwhelm, particularly those who have special needs, they can shut down or meltdown as their body becomes overwhelmed with stress chemicals. In these situations, children can sometimes seek out strong proprioceptive feedback to try to manage how their nervous system feels to them. Again, we can see the link back to the effects of caregiving on the development of the autonomic nervous system. Those learners who have been supported to manage this will appear 'naturally better' at behaving and regulating their emotions, when in fact what we are seeing is mainly a difference in their physiological reactions to stress.

Practical strategies for the classroom

My experiences suggest that emotional self-regulation is one of the areas where a lot of great work is already being done in classrooms. This is perhaps because emotions are such an obvious indicator to the teacher that 'something is wrong' with a learner, and that this might hamper their learning. We need to be sensitive about the work that we do as teachers around emotional regulation, particularly because of the links to adverse childhood experiences and potentially to safeguarding issues as well. It is tempting to assume that learners can easily and accurately name their emotions and describe them to us. There is a danger that they are putting a name to something because they believe that their teacher wants them to give a name to it, rather than offering an accurate reflection of what their emotions are. When we ask young people to express and explain their emotions, they need time to think about these in detail and to give considered responses.

An additional concern is that we need to be careful when we talk about 'managing' our emotions because we do not want to send the message to learners that emotions are somehow 'wrong' or to be avoided, i.e. to be suppressed. We need to make sure that children and young people understand that it is not a bad thing to feel – and to feel strongly – and even to 'sit with' an emotion so that we fully experience it. There is nothing wrong with feeling angry when someone does something to hurt you – the issue is about how you respond to that anger, and not with the anger itself. Sadness can be a natural and restorative emotion, as well as a troubling one, and it is therefore important that we approach this topic delicately and sensitively.

We should regularly remind learners that emotions come on a continuum, from negative to positive. When we talk about regulating emotions, we should make it clear that we are thinking about the positive feelings that we can have as well as more difficult ones that we might need to handle. The key question is how we can keep ourselves mainly calm, happy, feeling good about our lives and having a positive sense of self. Bear in mind that this is difficult for adults to achieve, let alone for young people, and particularly for teenagers, where hormones and other physiological changes can have a powerful impact on mood and emotions. You can find lots of thoughts about practical strategies to incorporate in your classroom in the sections that follow.

Noticing and describing emotions

Using language to notice and describe the emotions that we are feeling is a great practical first step in helping us to model how to manage our emotions – we need the vocabulary to describe what is going on for us inside in order to be able to manage it. This involves encouraging learners to 'tune into' the interoceptive information that their bodies are giving them, to identify what this information is 'saying' and to find the most accurate language with which to express what they are feeling. In turn, this puts them in a position to explore, examine and manage their emotions as necessary, and to better understand the emotions that others might be communicating to them in turn. Use the strategies below to start to explore emotions with your learners and to build their emotional literacy and self-regulation skills:

- ✓ Encourage your learners to be able to recognise and name at least six basic emotions, i.e. happy, angry, sad, scared, worried, bored. It is helpful to actively practise the faces that we make when we feel these things. Encourage your learners to look at each other's facial expressions and to identify the emotion that they are portraying.
- ✓ Talk about the kinds of things that might make children and young people feel these different emotions. Discuss the things that they could choose as an alternative to 'acting out' or getting upset when they feel this way. You might role-play some situations to explore 'what a good one looks like' (WAGOLL) and, equally, 'what a bad one looks like' (WABOLL).
- ✓ Help your learners notice their emotions by describing them to the children in clear terms, including information about the external visual indicators that we tend to see when emotions are being expressed – 'I notice that you seem to be getting annoyed because you are clenching your fists. Is that right?'
- ✓ Show learners images of people with a range of ages, cultural backgrounds, and occupations talking about the emotions that they can identify and how they can tell that these people are feeling this way.
- ✓ Ask learners to notice what they are feeling and to identify where they are feeling it in their body. They might talk about where in their body is feeling tense or funny – where the feeling seems to 'sit'.
- ✓ Encourage learners to name the feeling and to respond to it – is it a feeling that they want to sit with, overcome or manage, or do they want help to get it to dissipate?
- ✓ Mirrors are very useful to allow learners to identify their emotions – what does their face look like it is doing and how does this link to what they are feeling? Remember that children with autism might be feeling a different emotion internally to that which they express externally.
- ✓ Think about emotions in advance – ask learners to write down something that is bothering them – for instance, having a row with their parent before they left home – and then explore what it was and why it felt problematic. This can also help you to identify who in your class might be likely to be in a tricky mood and therefore may need some additional flexibility.

Identifying and exploring emotions

Some young people have issues with interoception, where they are not sufficiently tuned into what their bodies are telling them. Others will not have the vocabulary to accurately identify how their emotions can be described. There are plenty of strategies that teachers can use to offer a range of descriptive words for learners to build their emotional vocabulary and their emotional literacy, and to offer opportunities to engage in thinking about and analysing emotions:

- ✓ Build the vocabulary of emotions with your class by identifying different 'shades' and levels of various standard emotions – a bit like those colour charts where you see a variety of shades of the same colour. When we say that we are happy, we might mean that we are content, joyful, pleased, ecstatic or elated – explore the nuances between each one. Demonstrate that emotions are subtle things and that they can come in many nuanced gradations.
- ✓ Encourage your learners to consider the size of any problems about which they feel emotional – is it a small glitch, a medium-sized problem or a big worry? The size of the emotion will help to identify the solution to handling the issue. Many small glitches can easily be fixed by the person themselves, whereas you should encourage learners to always share with you if they have a big worry in their minds.
- ✓ When a meltdown has occurred, and with the child's permission, you might explore the difference between the *size* of the problem and the *size* of the emotional reaction. Reflecting might help them to adjust the size of their reaction the next time around. Some people use emotion thermometers or charts to talk about this.
- ✓ Choose stories that show how emotions can change, identifying how a character feels at the start and at the end of the story. What happened to them that elicited this change in their emotional state? How might your learners have felt in a similar situation?

Considering other sensory inputs

As we have explored in this chapter, interoceptive input is not only limited to helping us to understand our emotions; it also helps us to interact with our environment and stay safe in other ways. So we can learn to 'read' our bodies to find out whether we are feeling uncomfortable because we are too hot or too cold; we can understand that our mood is affected by hunger and that we need to eat something to increase our blood sugar levels; we can come to understand that inactivity and being still for too long is not good for us and is likely to lower our mood, so we remember to exercise to combat this. Key strategies for supporting the development of emotional self-regulation need to include an exploration of 'reading' all kinds of interoceptive information.

For example, primary teachers might have noticed that some learners appear unable to know when they are likely to be too hot or too cold, and they will rush outside into the playground without a coat on even when it is freezing cold. Similarly, some children appear to completely forget to eat, perhaps because they are not receiving sufficient interoceptive information to let them know that they are hungry. Support learners to build the skill of being able to 'read' their bodies in response to external environmental inputs, by using the following strategies:

- ✓ Talk with children to help them understand how and why they need to choose the appropriate clothing for different environmental conditions, and how they can warm themselves up and cool themselves down.
- ✓ Give learners access to sensory experiences so that their bodies can start to 'read' the information about aspects such as hot/cold – for instance, doing an activity with some ice blocks and encouraging your class to talk about how the ice feels against their skin.
- ✓ Give vocabulary to help your learners understand how to measure and describe the sensory feedback that they are getting. For instance, if a child falls over in the playground, you might say 'That looks sore' and ask 'Is it a little hurt or a big hurt?'

With older learners, some school policies can ironically mitigate against them assessing their own physical state and responding to it. If your school has a policy requiring blazers to always be worn, or insisting that additional layers of clothing must not be used even when it is cold, then it is worth challenging this based on the evidence. You might explain the likely impact on learners building an understanding of proprioceptive feedback and how this links to self-regulation skills.

Strategies for managing emotions

Ideally, we want our learners to be able to manage their emotions *before* they get to the point where they become completely dysregulated. By incorporating lots of opportunities to calm themselves and pinpoint emotions before they become overwhelming, you will support your learners to develop the skill of emotional regulation. The strategies described below are typically pre-emptive ones that can be put in place *before* issues occur, to support the development of emotional self-regulation in your learners:

- ✓ Mindfulness activities have been shown to help calm the brain and help people manage their emotional state, as well as supporting attentional control, as we saw in the previous chapter. These activities make a great start or end to the day, either setting learners up in a good state of mind or allowing them to leave feeling calm and positive. Encourage learners to observe and accept their feelings during mindfulness activities, rather than to try to dismiss or remove them.

- ✓ Create a calm zone in your classroom, somewhere that children can go when they are feeling over-stimulated. Typically, calm zones feature lower light levels (perhaps by using a small tent) and ways to ensure lower noise levels, such as listening to calming music through headphones. Although this would be tricky in a secondary context, what secondary schools can do is offer a 'time out' card for learners to use and create a 'time out' environment that will help to calm the learner down.
- ✓ Offer physical resources to act as an outlet for strong emotions – for instance, encouraging a child to blow up a balloon when they feel themselves getting wound up, giving them a cushion that they can bash when they feel their anger rising or using a resource that they can squash to take out their frustration.
- ✓ Encourage your class to try out 'volcano breathing'. Using the metaphor of a volcano, explain to the learners that if we do not let our emotions out but instead bottle them up, what can happen is that we get a sudden explosion. In the same way that a volcano can suddenly explode, sending out streams of lava, their emotions can explode too.
- ✓ Encourage learners to spend longer breathing out (around five seconds) than they do breathing in (around two seconds), to help calm them and avoid them hyperventilating. Ask your learners to visualise themselves letting out the emotions as they breathe out, but gradually. Just as a volcano can limit the force of an eruption by letting out small amounts of magma or steam, so too can your learners limit the force of their emotions.
- ✓ Research shows that deliberately making the facial expression associated with an emotion can trigger the part of the brain that lights up when we have that emotion. To cheer your class up, have a smiling contest with them, asking 'Who can make the biggest smile?'

Emotions check

It is tempting to assume that our learners come to us emotionally stable and ready to learn. Obviously, this is not going to be the case for all the learners in a class, and indeed it might only be the case for a small handful. In a secondary school context, where learners are moving from subject to subject and lesson to lesson, teachers will be aware that a negative experience earlier on can colour a young person's emotions for the rest of the day. For instance, when a class has just come from a lesson with a supply teacher, where there were issues with disruption and negative behaviours, this can create tension and overspill into the following lesson or lessons. Find ways to help you calm and settle a class by giving the learners time to think about, measure and identify their current emotional state. Respond to this information by adapting your approaches to the lesson – for instance, using a calming activity to settle a class if the learners seem agitated.

- ✓ Use an emotions gauge for learners to identify what their emotions are – for example, setting out a series of different-coloured pots, linked to different emotions, and asking the learners to put their names into the pot that links to their current emotional state as they enter the room. Putting the names on lolly sticks allows each learner to 'own' their emotion. This can give you a handy overview of the overall emotional 'temperature' of a class, to see how they are feeling as they arrive.
- ✓ You can also use names with Velcro® for learners to self-register under a range of emotion options. Again, this should give you a sense of how the overall feeling is within the group at the start of the day, which you can then talk about or react to through specific activities.
- ✓ Another way in which to gauge emotions is to have a slider on desks, with an arrow for learners to move up and down the scale, as they move between feeling calm and relaxed towards feeling like they are about to explode. Encourage learners to ask for support if their arrow is moving in the wrong direction.
- ✓ For older learners, where these strategies might not feel appropriate, a quick 'emotions check-in' using thumbs up, level or down can give you an idea about how everyone is feeling. It is also often possible to gauge the mood of a class as they enter the room by reading the non-verbal signals that they are communicating.

Scaffolding emotions

Just as with the subject-based curriculum, a key strategy for supporting emotional self-regulation is to help the learner find suitable scaffolds that will help them manage their emotions. For example, if a learner repeatedly gets frustrated as they approach a series of questions that they find difficult, we might scaffold this by:

- ✓ Acknowledging that we can see that the learner is struggling with their emotions in response to the difficulties, making it clear that we are here to offer support but also that we believe in the learner and we think that they can cope with the challenge with our help.
- ✓ Praising the learner for the way in which they are managing a frustrating task – for instance, acknowledging that we can see that they are keeping going at it, even though they are finding it difficult.

- ✓ Helping the learner with the first question and then saying that we will come back to see how they are getting on in a little while. For a very anxious learner, we might even specify the amount of time before we return – for instance, by turning over a sand-timer and saying that we will come back before it runs out.
- ✓ Suggesting that they take a 'brain break' – for instance, getting a drink of water if they feel themselves starting to become overwhelmed.

We can also scaffold for learners by building up the difficulty gradually, starting with a set of problems that we know they will find relatively easy to solve and then introducing a slightly more difficult task. Scaffolding can also help you to calm a group down, as well as help learners handle negative emotions – for instance, using your voice to calm an over-excited class.

The role of the teacher

We need to be conscious that, as the saying goes, 'we make the weather' in our classrooms or teaching spaces. Our approach as educators will have a direct impact on the moods and emotions of the children and young people with whom we work. In terms of emotional regulation, we are constantly modelling 'what a good one looks like' (and probably 'what a bad one looks like' too). When we show our learners that it is possible to respond to external pressures by staying calm, cool and collected, and not getting overly upset or frustrated, we are modelling the attitude that we hope that they will eventually achieve for themselves. Interestingly, even just *forcing* yourself to laugh has been shown to lead to a greater feeling of contentment and happiness over time – the emotion does not have to be authentic and deeply felt to have an impact (Šimić et al., 2021).

We can also demonstrate what happens when we *do* lose emotional control, using our own inability to fully regulate our emotions as an example of how no one is perfect, that we can all reflect and develop, and of 'what not to do'. We need to be willing to acknowledge our loss of emotional self-regulation and to apologise for any negative impact that this has had. For instance, if we shouted at the class because they made us angry with their behaviour, it is perfectly possible to admit that we should not have shouted. This does not mean that we are saying that the behaviours were not wrong in the first place – just that we could have chosen a better reaction to the difficult emotions that they elicited in us.

We can even encourage our learners to support us in managing our own emotional regulation by asking them what they could do to help us stay calm in the future – in other words, how they can help us to reflect on and reappraise our emotions to approach the situation differently next time around. Although it is tempting to tell a class that they effectively 'made you' lose your temper because of their poor behaviour, this kind of passing of the blame is not useful. Some key strategies for teachers to consider that best support emotional self-regulation are given below:

- ✓ Although it is important to immediately support a learner who is emotionally dysregulated, we can also allow learners time to sit with their emotions where appropriate. The idea is to allow them to experience the emotion, rather than jumping in immediately to try to calm them down or cheer them up. Be conscious of your instinct to potentially over-help your learners because you do not want to see them upset.
- ✓ Send the message (consciously and subconsciously) that it is fine to experience emotions, but that we can also consider reframing the situations in which we find ourselves so that we experience them as less upsetting or stressful. Emphasise that the learners have agency to choose how to manage their emotional state.
- ✓ Ask the question 'What could we do differently next time?' to encourage learners to plan for progress in managing their emotions. Where possible, spend time talking through the options with your class. This could be a useful activity for tutor time or in PSHE (personal, social, health and economic education) lessons.
- ✓ Scaffold the learning around emotional regulation in a similar way to that in which we might scaffold the learning in curriculum subjects. Scaffolds could include breaking challenges down into small steps, suggesting appropriate targets and timings, utilising one-to-one support or using resources to help manage a situation.
- ✓ Maintain appropriate levels of challenge and then find ways in which to coach and support learners through the things that they find difficult or challenging, rather than under-doing the levels of challenge to avoid 'upsetting' your learners. Remember that trying, struggling and failing can be emotionally uncomfortable for us but that they play a crucial role in learning.
- ✓ Support learners to replace an ineffective response to difficult stimuli (a completely dysregulated response) with a more effective response, where they acknowledge that something is difficult emotionally but they find other ways in which to manage or cope with it.

Prosody and emotional regulation

When we think about how our own approaches and behaviours as educators can support emotional regulation, it is important to consider the ways in which we speak to our learners. The regions in our brains that process emotions also react to sound. One of the key parts of the brain that deals with emotions is called the amygdala, which is very sensitive indeed to sounds and music. (This is one of the reasons why music has the power to elicit such strong emotions in us.) This part of our brains also links our emotions to memories, learning and the senses. From a very early age, at around seven months old, babies show sensitivity to the human voice and the way in which it conveys emotions (Grossman et al., 2010). If you think for a moment about how other people's voices can affect you and even impact your emotional state, it is clear that voice is a powerful factor in our subconscious reactions to others. The parts of the brain that handle emotion are highly sensitive to prosody, or the patterns of stresses and intonations in our voices. This means that our learners will pick up a lot of information about our emotional state from how we sound. Learn to step outside yourself and hear yourself as an external observer would hear you, becoming aware of how your voice is betraying any negative emotions and how it can be used to give emotional warmth to a situation. The strategies given below will help you to manage the sound of your voice:

- ✓ Be aware of your voice rising in pitch if you become stressed. If you become aware of tension, pause, take some deep breaths and then relax your neck, particularly around the larynx area. This will help you to drop the pitch of your voice.
- ✓ Take care about your voice rising in volume if you start to feel a loss of emotional control. Pause, take a breath and imagine yourself dropping the volume as though quickly turning a speaker down.
- ✓ Make a point of slightly over-emphasising your vocal tone, since it is a particularly important aspect of voice usage when thinking about the emotional responses that we want to elicit in our classrooms.
- ✓ Aim to make the tone of your voice match the emotion that you want to express to learners, whether this is kindly, warm, interested/curious, disappointed and so on.
- ✓ If possible, take some recordings of yourself so that you can listen back to your voice when the learners are not around. We often find that we sound remarkably different to how we *think* that we sound when we do this.

A very interesting recent study into teachers' use of voice confirmed that teacher prosody has a significant impact on the emotions of learners (Paulmann and Weinstein, 2023). The research explored how children felt when they heard different tones of voice from teachers. When they heard a controlling tone of voice, one that was pressuring or demanding, the learners expected to feel lower satisfaction regarding their psychological needs, lower wellbeing and lower self-esteem. Interestingly, controlling voices also made learners less likely to share information with teachers, both positive information regarding their achievements and also negative information such as that they were being bullied. The research found that the most effective tones of voice were autonomy-supportive, encouraging a sense of relatedness and personal agency. In other words, by focusing on sounding warm and supportive, teachers can create learning environments that better support students' needs and wellbeing. This ties into the synchrony described at the start of this chapter – it can really help us to build our own emotional regulation where we feel that sense of a 'bond' with others.

Managing our own emotions

When I work with new teachers, one of the things that I often say to them is that they need to learn to regulate their *own* behaviours in order to have the best chance of managing the behaviour of their classes. A lot of the best advice about becoming a teacher, and about relating to children and young people, is about first regulating yourself. There are lots of potential stressors in the average classroom. Teachers are making thousands – if not tens of thousands – of decisions a day and they must constantly react to and deal with unexpected events. Inappropriate behaviour naturally makes us feel defensive because it seems like an 'attack' on the efforts that we put in for our learners.

Remember too that you need to deal with your own emotions before trying to support children in handling theirs. In many classroom situations where a learner is emotional, the adult may well be feeling emotional too. Clearly, we can use very similar approaches to managing our own emotions to those strategies that work for our learners. These might involve:

- ✓ distancing yourself momentarily from the emotionally difficult situation – for example, by looking out of the window to remind yourself that 'there is a world out there'
- ✓ pausing to calm yourself down by breathing deeply until your heart rate slows
- ✓ reminding yourself to retain a perspective – although we may feel defensive, it is rare that a learner's behaviour is actually personal.

Supporting emotionally dysregulated learners

One of the temptations when handling children's emotions is to immediately step in to 'solve' the emotional upset for the learner. This is entirely understandable – it is never nice to see someone upset, especially when that person is a child. However, it is important to remember that when a young person is dysregulated, they are not in the right mental position to take on board your advice. Their brain is over-activated and unable to make sense of our rational inputs. When a learner is emotionally dysregulated:

- ✓ Do not immediately step in and try to problem-solve on their behalf by suggesting lots of solutions.
- ✓ First, acknowledge that they are upset. Be open to what the child is experiencing, perhaps describing it or clarifying that you understand that the situation is difficult for them.
- ✓ You might say something like 'That must be very hard to handle' or 'I can see why you would find that really difficult'.
- ✓ Focus on describing the emotion that you can see, rather than trying to explain it away or stop it from happening. You could say something such as, 'I can imagine that you are feeling very upset/angry/annoyed by that.'
- ✓ Encourage the child or young person to find ways in which to manage their emotional reaction, particularly the physical aspects of it, which can lead to issues such as hyperventilating – for instance, by saying 'Let's breathe together to help you to calm down.'
- ✓ If you are working with young children, you might offer physical comfort as appropriate to help them return to a state of calm – for instance, rubbing their back.
- ✓ Remember that regulating our emotions takes time because we need to get back to our rational brain and away from our emotional one. Do not rush the process to try to 'get on' with things.

Interestingly, a key part of our role as teachers is to understand when to intervene and when to step back and allow learners to experience a situation from which they will learn. A key question to ask ourselves is about the 'zone of proximal development' (Vygotsky, 1978). We want learning to be just hard enough to provide challenge and progression, but not so hard as to provoke panic or for the learners to feel overwhelmed, and this includes emotional regulation. It is important to be aware that it is hard for us not to be tempted to over-help and over-intervene in situations where learners are struggling to regulate their emotions.

Once you have acknowledged the validity of the child's emotion and they have returned to a relatively calm and regulated state, you can then talk about how you might problem-solve the situation together. You can also plan for how you might try to avoid the same situation arising in the future. Model strategies for self-regulation and metacognition by narrating what you are thinking – for example, by saying:

- ✓ 'Let me write that down, so I don't forget', where a learner is furious about a perceived injustice.
- ✓ 'I'm just going to take a moment to calm myself down', where both you and the learner have got into a heated state.

✓ 'Let's have a think about what happened. Can you help me to understand what triggered those feelings for you?'

By taking metacognitive approaches to all aspects of self-regulation, we essentially model for our learners that it is possible to involve the rational parts of our brains in supporting us to better handle our emotional reactions and responses to the difficulties that we encounter.

Chapter 8
Supporting the Development of Empathy

In this chapter, we will:

- ✓ Examine how empathy develops, identifying the timing in relation to overall self-regulation.
- ✓ Understand more about 'theory of mind' and why this is essential for empathy.
- ✓ Think about the role of stories and the imagination in the development of empathy.
- ✓ Explore what self-distancing is and how it can help learners to build empathy.
- ✓ Learn strategies to help to support the development of empathy in the classroom.

The development of empathy is a fascinating aspect of self-regulation because it requires us to make an astounding imaginative leap. Not only do we have to position ourselves in the mind of another human being, to see how the world feels and appears to them, but we must also put aside our own thoughts, feelings and emotions to help us to understand how someone can hold entirely different beliefs to our own. It is useful to remember that empathy is one of the later developing self-regulation skills. Although we see it referred to in curricula from the Early Years, even adults can sometimes struggle with this aspect of self-regulation. Indeed, if we look at the increasing divide between different 'camps' of people that has arisen, particularly on social media and in politics, it could be argued that adults have got *worse* at demonstrating empathy in recent years.

There are many reasons why empathy is such a key skill for us to help learners to develop. When I work with teachers on their approaches to behaviour, it tends to be one of the first skills that they mention as being important as a behavioural skill. Empathy allows us to see the world from a range of perspectives and to better understand how other people experience their lives. Empathy also plays a critical part in ensuring appropriate behaviour in the classroom because once we understand how our own behaviours make other people feel and the impact that our behaviour can have on others, we can hopefully start to make conscious choices about behaving differently to alleviate the potential negative effects.

As teachers, we are in a privileged position when it comes to helping our learners build empathy because we have lots of ways to 'get at' this aspect of self-regulation. For example, in a drama class or through role-play activities, we can actively get young people to take on the characters of others. This is effectively the first step in the imaginative leap required to develop empathy. In an English class or at storytime, we can think about the characters that we meet in stories, how they feel in different situations and how we know this. In a history lesson, we can use biographies and historical artefacts to help our learners think about how people from history experienced and felt about their world. Empathy offers a very rich furrow to plough when thinking about opportunities within the curriculum.

The development of empathy

The ability to empathise emerges and develops during infancy and childhood, with strong links to the quality of early caregiving, in a similar way to the development of emotional self-regulation. Although empathy takes time to fully develop, the first signs of empathy appear early in life. We might not think that it would be possible for babies to show empathy, but research has shown that crying is 'contagious' and that newborns will cry in response to the cries of other babies, particularly when the cry sounds distressed (Geangu et al., 2010). As discussed in the previous chapter, babies can 'tune into' the feelings and thinking of adults early on. Through high-quality 'serve and return' interactions, babies develop synchrony, or emotional attunement, with their caregivers. Babies can identify the difference between a responsive, emotionally attuned face and one that is blank and expressionless. They also know to focus on the eyes of their caregivers, showing a preference for people who make eye contact.

These signs indicate the early development of empathy, and the more that the caregivers interact with their infants, the more the baby learns to tune into them. By about two months of age, a baby might already have learned to smile at their parents or carers – the baby has effectively learned that they can make their caregivers happy, that happiness is beneficial and what 'being happy' looks like. Gradually, children develop more complex empathetic behaviours – for example, through their pretend play. When children – or a child and an adult – pretend together, they must tune into each other's ideas and intentions, cooperating and considering how they can take on different roles. Where young children engage in plenty of social play, this supports the development of perspective-taking skills and, consequently, the development of empathy.

As with so many human behaviours, empathy appears to be an evolutionary adaptation, which has developed to ensure our survival. Being empathetic helps us to build social connections and to work more effectively in groups. As might be expected, research has shown that experiences of chronic stress in a child's early years may negatively impact the development of empathy (Levy et al., 2019). It is also the case that when a mother experiences post-natal depression (PND), this can be linked to children showing reduced empathetic behaviours (Murray et al., 2019). Mothers with PND may be focused on themselves and thus find it difficult to focus on their baby and to respond intuitively to their interactions. There may also be reduced touching and fewer signs of affection. It may also be the case that parenting difficulties can arise because a baby is difficult to console – the development of early relationships is a complex, bidirectional process.

Empathy and theory of mind

Children demonstrate some understanding of other people's minds early on, noticing that others might have different preferences, goals or intentions to themselves. For instance, research has shown that young children understand when someone might prefer one food over another, and they understand that they should offer them more of the preferred food. Young children start to imitate and mimic the people around them, again showing that they seem to understand that other people's minds might work differently from their own. Children also learn to pay attention to the things on which others are focusing, demonstrating an understanding that someone else might be interested in something different to them.

Gradually, children learn what is called 'visual perspective taking', where they understand that other people see things in the world from alternative visual perspectives and that from their own viewpoint, the world will not appear the same as from another's. In other words, something that is visible to one person might be hidden from another, depending on where they are positioned. This is, of course, the basis of any successful game of hide and seek. Gradually, children come to learn that other people can have false beliefs, as in the theory of mind experiment described in Chapter 1 (see pages 11–12), forming the basis of their emerging understanding of other people's minds.

In a classroom context, we can see that our learners need to have developed 'theory of mind' in order to empathise with peers and school staff because it helps them to understand how others view and experience their inappropriate behaviours. Because theory of mind helps us to see that other people can have beliefs, intentions, feelings and wishes that are different to our own, it also allows us to start to predict and interpret their behaviours. This helps us to figure out people's motivations more fully, which, in turn, allows us to form more cooperative relationships. This is why, when a learner behaves inappropriately towards someone, teachers will often ask, 'How do you think so-and-so felt when you did that?' We are effectively asking learners to place themselves in the mind of another and to consider how their own behaviour feels in the light of what they imagine.

The research suggests that our theory of mind changes over time, starting to come into place at around the age of four years old, but adapting and developing as we age (Korkmaz, 2011). The way in which we make sense of other people's mental states also appears to change over time, in response to our experiences and our social interactions. Theory of mind allows us to become gradually more adept at navigating social situations and building positive relationships, as we learn to see the world from other people's viewpoints. It is also closely linked to the development of impulse control, probably because we start to think about how our impulses might impact others. Alongside all this, there are also connections to moral development and values-based education. As well as understanding that others might experience the world differently from the way in which we do, we need to believe that it is *important* to treat others properly too.

One of the ways in which we learn to 'read' other people's internal thoughts and emotions is through interpreting their facial expressions. When people are highly skilled at interpreting what others are feeling, they are likely to be more adept at forming social relationships. Interestingly, research seems to suggest that children with autism develop theory of mind later than other children, and this, in turn, means that they find it harder to interpret how others might be thinking and feeling. They are less able to 'read' other people's emotions and thoughts by interpreting the outward signals and repositioning themselves into someone else's perspective. This appears to link to the difficulties that children with autism can have in understanding figurative and metaphorical language. To be able to 'get' how something like a metaphor or a sarcastic comment works, we must understand that people can interpret the world in different ways according to how they see it or the beliefs that they have about it – in other words, that they are not always being literal in how they express what they see.

Educators and empathy

Teachers and educators typically become very adept at understanding their learners' minds and empathising with them. We are constantly stepping into other people's shoes because our professional lives involve a great deal of reflection from perspectives outside of our own. We reflect on what worked in our classrooms for the learners, why it worked and why some learners struggled with something while others found it easy. We also regularly reflect on our own behaviours, particularly when there is a difficult moment or the class does not 'get' something that we have tried to explain.

Empathy is at the heart of building positive relationships in the classroom because it shows a willingness to reposition ourselves into another's experience of the world. When I talk with teachers about their own school experiences, it is striking how many of them will describe a teacher who 'believed in them' or who 'really cared about them'. Often, the student went on to study a subject to the highest level because of the belief and trust demonstrated in the relationship that their teacher built with them. This sense of emotional attunement with a teacher seems to mirror the kind of responsive input that early caregivers can give, which, in turn, supports the development of emotional self-regulation and empathy.

A very useful approach to support yourself in building empathy in your classroom is to literally *sit in your learners' shoes* by *sitting in their seats* when they are not in the room. Step outside of your teacher self and physically reposition yourself to see your classroom from the learners' perspective. It is useful to sit in several different positions in your room, as your viewpoint and experience of the space are likely to be different from each one. Consider what draws your attention – the questions below should act as a useful starting point:

- ✓ How do you feel in the space – what is your emotional reaction to the room?
- ✓ What differences are there between the learner's perspective and the teacher's perspective?
- ✓ What would be the first thing to which you would pay attention here?
- ✓ Looking around the room, what might distract you from your learning?
- ✓ How connected would you feel with the teacher from this position in the room?
- ✓ What do you notice about the physical environment? Is it comfy/uncomfy? Is it too hot/cold?
- ✓ How might you feel about the person whom you sit next to? Is there space for both of you to work comfortably?

Learning empathy through narratives

It is interesting to consider the power of narratives in supporting learning and understanding, and how this links to the ideas of emotional self-regulation, attunement and empathy that are explored in this and the previous chapter. Psychologists sometimes refer to stories or narratives as being 'psychologically privileged' – this means that they are treated differently to other types of material in the human mind and in our memories. Stories help us to process and understand a specific context because they trigger the imagination – we can learn to picture ourselves 'inside' the story. Stories also help us to link new ideas to what we already know, building a coherent schema of concepts that are based on and extend our existing understanding.

Stories are one of the most powerful ways in which we can help children to learn (and especially to learn to empathise). Indeed, stories are so fundamental to learning that they are one of the rare areas of education where everyone agrees – stories really do matter. We should all read and discuss stories with our learners, as well as encourage children to read for their own pleasure. A wonderful way in which to build empathy is through exploring stories and talking about what happens to the people who inhabit them because it helps learners place themselves in the minds of the characters. In the imaginative worlds of stories, characters must face challenges, cope with difficulties, demonstrate self-control and so on. By discussing the various ways that characters feel in different situations, how they handle their emotions and the challenges that they face, we show our learners that it is possible to be resilient, even in the most difficult or challenging of situations.

Putting ourselves 'in the shoes of' a character in a story, whether real or imagined, links closely to the concept of self-distancing discussed in Chapter 5 (see pages 69–70). It allows us to gain a better perspective on our own lives – for example, when we read about a child in difficult circumstances, this might help us to reflect on our own advantages. Research seems to show that stories may help to support empathy where they foster in-group/out-group identification and avoid in-group/out-group bias (Kucirkova, 2019). In other words, although we normally empathise more closely with members of what we perceive as 'our group', stories can help us to better understand and offer rational compassion to members of a group with whom we do not normally identify.

The more that we can immerse ourselves in the story world and identify with the characters in a story, the more that reading or listening to a story becomes a continuous exercise in building empathy for us. Although we cannot change the outcome of the story, we can still feel the pain or joy of the characters and live in their world vicariously for a while. In an experiment into empathy in the 1970s, researchers found that the attitudes of White children towards Black children improved significantly when they heard a story where the main protagonist was a Black child (Katz and Zalk, 1978). A more recent review into how imagining other perspectives can help with intergroup relations noted that empathy was often a feature of conflict-resolution situations (Batson and Ahmad, 2009). This supports the idea that building empathy is also about improving equity, and that as such it deserves our attention and focus in terms of its contribution to a values-based education.

There is plenty of evidence (e.g. Firth, 2015) to suggest that the quality of the stories matters, and that for stories to support the development of empathy, they need to be able to 'transport' the reader into the story. Researchers found that the stories that do this best are those that have a powerful dramatic arc – stories that create the dramatic tension needed to help the reader feel absorbed in the story. As the story holds the audience's attention and they associate with the characters, stress hormones get released. These, in turn, increase the heart and respiration rate of the reader – that feeling of being 'gripped' by a powerful story and desperate to know 'what happens next'. The researchers found that it was the hormone oxytocin that does this – the same hormone that makes people more generous, trustworthy and compassionate. Great stories can help people to read social cues more effectively and encourage them to become better advocates for others.

Remember that stories do not have to be fictional to support the development of empathy – the power of a biographical or autobiographical story may elicit more feelings of empathy than a fictional one because it is so obviously about a real-life situation. When we think about the influence of role models in the lives of our learners, we can see how powerful these 'influencers' can be on children and young people's behaviours. The narratives that teachers use in class about their own lives are also powerful for building empathy. Many of us will have seen how powerful it is to share an anecdote to illustrate a point or to help learners see how a concept applies in a real-life context. When we think about something that happened to someone whom we know, this gives the narrative more immediacy and veracity.

Practical strategies for the classroom

As we saw above, the use of stories and narratives is one of the key practical ways in which teachers can help support the development of empathy in their learners. Clearly, this is not a simple fix – these skills develop over a long period and we might only have limited time with any group of learners. However, this is all part of building a picture in the learners' minds about what the options are and how it might be possible to become more empathetic towards others. In the primary classroom, stories will form an integral part of the daily routine, with class story-time or whole-class story-reading on a regular basis. In secondary classrooms, it is worth thinking about where in the curriculum stories and narratives might be utilised. Although we tend to associate them with drama or English lessons, they will be just as valid in a history lesson when thinking about real-life characters. We might also use biographical narratives in lessons such as art or science to think about the lives of key historical figures, or anecdotes in PSHE to bring the learning to life.

When we are considering different ways in which to use the power of story in our classrooms, there are plenty of possibilities to consider:

- ✓ role plays in which the learners 'take on' a character with specific attributes
- ✓ drama activities such as 'conscience alley', where the learners become the 'thoughts' inside a character's head
- ✓ immersive story-reading in which we encourage learners to 'act out' parts of a story
- ✓ writing in role as a person from history, to think about their perspective on events
- ✓ watching video stories from other countries to better understand different cultures and communities
- ✓ retelling and updating stories to see how they reflect modern-day concerns, as well as those when they were written
- ✓ using storyboarding techniques and creating comic book stories.

Modelling empathy

As with any kind of learning, one of the best ways in which teachers can help children learn the skill of empathy is through modelling it for them. There is a great deal of research that shows the effect of relationships – particularly child-carer relationships – and how children will imitate the models that they see around them (e.g. Carlo et al., 2017). For instance, where a parent is responsive, non-punitive and non-authoritarian in their child-rearing practices, their children will have higher levels of affective and cognitive empathy and prosocial behaviours. Even the youngest children can engage in some complex discussions around the effects of their behaviour on others, particularly if we regularly model the language and frame the discussion for them. Look at 'Aldie and Mamma' having a bedtime conversation on YouTube (Aldiebears Adventures, 2023) to see just how complex a four-year-old's discussion of emotions can be. This exchange between Aldie and his mum very clearly shows how repeatedly modelling empathetic language can support the development of empathy, even in the youngest children.

By being responsive to learners in class, being aware of how their emotions influence them and understanding their different perspectives, we can demonstrate 'what empathy looks like'. We model empathy (or fail to model it) in all our interactions with learners, particularly around the ways in which we handle and support them when they are struggling. A key aspect of this modelling is to think about how you use language to frame situations where your learners are struggling to regulate and cooperate with you. Consider how the language that you use can demonstrate to a learner that you are actively listening and empathising with them.

This will make it more likely that they will be able to return to a regulated state. For instance:

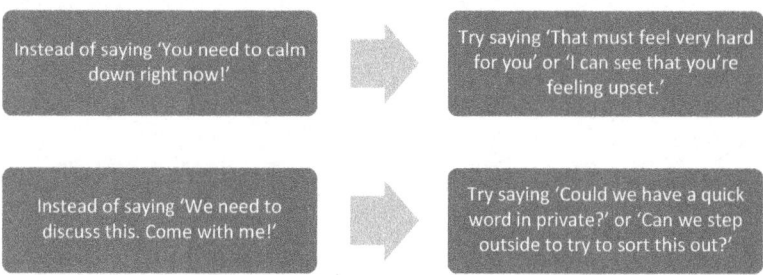

Again, the first step in achieving this ability to reframe our discussions with learners is to learn to regulate our own emotions. This can be incredibly difficult in the heat of a tricky classroom situation, but a good first step is to remember to pause, calm yourself and breathe *before* you interact with a learner about inappropriate behaviour.

'Caring for' activities

A key aspect of empathy is around caring for others – we need to support our learners to feel emotionally 'attuned' to other living things. For some children, this emotional attunement has been their experience from an early age, with their carers at home and in the other settings that they have attended. We can hear this emotional attunement demonstrated in the way in which carers 'tune into' their baby's emotions, matching the pitch of their voice to their baby's happy squeal. Gradually, with repeated experiences of emotional attunement, babies and young children come to understand that other people can and will join in with and mirror their feelings when they express them. Similarly, as we saw in the last chapter, where teachers 'tune into' their learners and use a warm, responsive-sounding tone of voice in class, this, in turn, impacts the likelihood of learners feeling that they can open up to them. They perceive that their teacher 'cares for' them.

Unfortunately, some children will not have had the same experiences of emotional attunement to others – in fact, you can probably sense where this applies to learners in your classroom, who struggle to model the kind of empathetic and caring attitudes that we would hope to see and which support better behaviour. However, it is possible to support them in developing these skills with practice and time. To help our learners build the skill of attunement, we need to both demonstrate caring to them and give them chances to care for other people and other living things. This supports the development of empathy and builds a sense of trust and responsibility. We might ask our learners to care for:

- ✓ plants, in the classroom or in an outdoor space, seeing how their care helps the plants to grow well and to produce fruit, vegetables or flowers
- ✓ animals, such as a school dog, school chickens or a class pet such as a guinea pig or fish
- ✓ people, by raising money for charity, giving to those less fortunate than themselves or perhaps writing a piece from the viewpoint of the victim of a crime
- ✓ imaginary creatures, such as a class teddy that they take home at the weekends to write about their adventures.

Some settings have developed ongoing relationships – for instance, with a local care home – to support their learners in understanding how we can care for others and why we would want to do this. One of the keys to developing empathy is helping our learners to understand that, despite any differences in terms of culture, religion, appearance and so on, other people are also 'just like them' in many ways.

Find ways in which to help your learners understand each other's similarities and differences by getting them to do activities to group themselves in various ways, to show them that they have similarities to peers (for instance, the month in which they were born or how many languages they speak). Encourage learners to support each other's hopes and desires, building the idea that they can and should work together as a learning community. Think about how you group learners in your classroom – my advice would be to generate random groupings right from the start. This sends the message that 'we work with anyone and everyone'.

Positive trait attribution

Another straightforward strategy for the classroom that can help to build empathetic behaviours is 'positive trait attribution'. The idea behind this is to encourage learners to believe that they are *the kind of person* who naturally chooses to behave in moral and empathetic ways. This helps them to come to see themselves as a responsible person who can make good decisions around self-regulatory behaviours. So, when asking a learner to share a resource with another, we might say something like, 'I just know that you're the kind of generous person who is going to be able to share this with a partner.'

The way in which people attribute causes to both their positive and negative experiences can have a powerful impact on their sense of self. Again, this links to the idea of learners being active agents in their own behaviours and to the idea of encouraging a growth mindset. The aim should be to encourage our learners to attribute their success to the effort that they put into things to help them feel able to overcome challenges. Where they fail or struggle, we want them to see this as something caused by external factors, which they can fix. This is closely linked to the kind of language that we use, particularly around assessment of their learning. When using praise, we need to aim to praise the *effort* and the *approach*, rather than the outcomes and the work. The idea is to encourage learners to believe that they can choose to put in the hard work and that this will directly influence their outcomes. For example, when we are complimenting a learner's work, we might phrase this as something like:

- ✓ 'I really liked the way in which you kept going when you were struggling with that.'
- ✓ 'I think it was a real positive that you refused to get distracted and that you worked so hard to stay focused.'

Where some learners repeatedly experience punitive consequences for poor choices around behaviour, unfortunately, this can lead to a decrease in self-esteem and, consequently, to a sense of helplessness around making any changes to their behaviour. They can come to believe that there is 'something about them' that just makes them 'bad', rather than remembering that their behaviour is within their effortful control and that it is possible to change and develop. This links back to the idea of unconditional positive regard discussed in Chapter 1 and Chapter 4 of this book – our learners need to understand that we still care about them as people even when we do not like the behaviour that they have demonstrated.

Chapter 9
Goal Setting, Resilience and Agency

In this chapter, we will:

- ✓ Understand how goal-setting behaviours and agency develop.
- ✓ Consider different conceptualisations of childhood and the role of agency.
- ✓ Explore how we can support our learners to set themselves realistic goals.
- ✓ Consider how we can help learners to face challenges and failures with resilience.
- ✓ Examine the kind of classroom climate that supports learners to have agency.
- ✓ Think about how we can encourage responsibility in our learners.

One of the key features in the development of self-regulation is for children and young people to understand that their actions, their behaviour and their choices will have an impact on their experience of their world – that they can set themselves goals, work to achieve these and cope if they do not. We want our learners to feel safe and willing to take risks, make decisions and actively 'give it a go' when it comes to learning, and indeed when it comes to life – in other words, to have a strong sense of self and a belief in themselves as independently minded, capable people who have the agency to make good choices. This is particularly important for the development of self-regulation because we want our learners to consciously engage in self-regulatory behaviours. These behaviours include:

- adapting their actions to help themselves learn
- setting achievable goals
- reflecting on their progress
- managing their emotions.

A key facet of successful learning is being able to set ourselves goals, which we then work as active agents to achieve. Our learners need to be supported to learn how to set themselves realistic targets and how to manage their motivation to work towards these. As teachers, we are constantly setting goals for our learners, often framing these as 'learning objectives'. Ideally, though, we need children and young people to take over this process for themselves – to be active and involved as learners. Interestingly, we see this focus on active involvement in their own learning at opposite ends of the education system. Early Years settings prioritise children's agency, building on learners' interests and encouraging them to be as independent as possible; similarly, once learners reach sixth form, college or university, they are expected to take much more responsible agency in their own learning and to focus in on following their own interests.

When thinking about how to support goal-setting behaviours, we need to help young people learn how to handle situations in which they do not meet the targets that they have set for themselves or that others have set for them. A key factor in working towards any long-term learning goal is the ability to defer or delay gratification, explored earlier in this book. The ability to experience short-term discomfort or difficulty because of the goal of achieving a greater long-term aim links closely to positive outcomes. Our learners need to understand that they can handle challenges by being encouraged to do so and supported via co-regulation to cope if things go wrong. Interestingly, where learners are given agency to follow their own interests, they will choose more challenging activities than if they are simply complying with what someone else asks them to do.

The development of agency and goal-setting behaviours

One of the core factors in 'being human' is having a sense of agency – the belief that we can determine our own pathways, take responsibility for our decisions, set our own goals and, in turn, have an element of control over what happens to us and the outcomes that we achieve. Agency is not something that we can exercise in isolation – it happens in a relationship with an environment and with other people. It is mediated through our experiences and through the society in which we live. It is tricky to research the early development of agency since babies are non-verbal and this makes it difficult to know whether they are making active choices or not. However, research has shown that the perception of other people's actions as intentional develops during the first year of a child's life (Woodward, 2009). Children learn from past experiences where they have chosen to act and the outcomes of those experiences. Where adults are supportive of their attempts, offering scaffolds but not over-helping, children learn that trying and failing are essential for learning. For agency to develop, they must be given opportunities to make decisions, work towards goals and play an active role in their own daily lives and, consequently, their outcomes.

In a fascinating study into conscious awareness, researchers looked at how human beings learn to act with purpose (Sloan et al., 2023). They studied how babies reacted when their foot was tied to a mobile, meaning that they could consciously move it with their feet. A positive feedback loop effectively developed, whereby the more the mobile moved, the more the baby was stimulated to move, producing even more movement in the mobile. In other words, the babies seemed to understand that there was a cause-and-effect relationship between them and what happened with the mobile – they effectively set themselves a goal and made it happen. The researchers described an 'aha!' moment when the baby recognised that it was causing the movement. At this point, the babies transitioned from spontaneous behaviour to intentional behaviour, marked by a rapid increase in the baby's movement rate.

In another fascinating discovery, the researchers also noticed that the babies found meaning in both movement *and* stillness – they also chose to pause their movements and thus the mobile. The babies realised that they had the power to make things happen in the world intentionally – in other words, that they had agency, could set themselves goals and work to achieve them. As they develop, children shape their behaviours in response to the outcomes that they have come to expect – 'if I do this, then that will happen'. By around the age of three years old, research shows that children start to work towards outcomes that they value and that these motivate them more than outcomes that they do not value (Klossek et al., 2008). This is the start of their gradually emerging autonomy and agency in the pursuit of specific and self-directed goals. It seems that in the period between two and three years of age, there is a transition in behavioural control from understanding that a particular behaviour will generate an outcome, to learning that we can actively work towards a specific goal.

Conceptualising agency

Researchers (Manyukhina and Wyse, 2021) have described agency as 'the capacity to act', identifying the various elements of agency that work together to allow us to make choices and set ourselves goals: a personal *sense* of agency – the belief that we can act independently and make our own decisions; the *exercise* of agency – real-life opportunities to utilise our sense of agency; and *affordances* – the belief of learners that they are capable and can act on the opportunities that they are given. This means that part and parcel of agency is our interactions with our environment – it is socially mediated. Interestingly, while there is plenty of research into *teacher* agency, there is relatively little into *children's* agency in educational settings. This might tell us something about the focus within the system at present, and how children and young people are currently conceptualised within formal education.

Agency has been described as 'the power to originate action' (Code, 2020) – the ability to regulate and control our thinking, motivation and behaviours through our existing beliefs. This ability is often described using the term 'self-efficacy', a concept explored throughout this book and closely linked to self-regulation. In social cognitive theory, it is proposed that while the action of regulating ourselves is an individual endeavour, we do not operate in isolation – we can only do so in relation to other people and our environment. This theory conceptualises agency as being an interplay between intention, forethought, self-regulation and self-reflection. In other words:

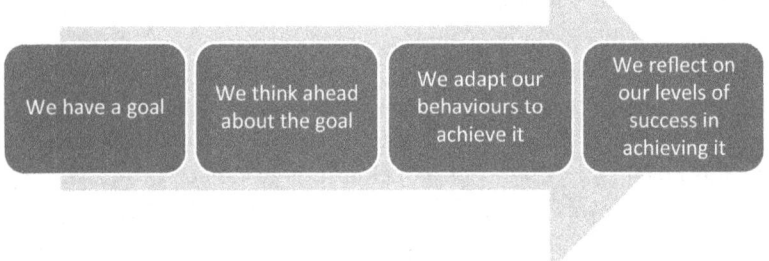

Again, in these definitions of agency, we can see the very close links between self-regulation and self-regulated learning. It is worth remembering that a sense of agency in our learning is not about working alone – a young person who actively wants to learn something will often reach out to others (including teachers or perhaps online materials) to support them.

If we do not have the sense that *it matters* what choices we make – that we are active agents in our own futures – then it is difficult to see why we would be motivated to do the right thing. We can see this writ large with those learners who constantly get into trouble in school – the system of sanctions just does not seem to 'work' for them; they get the same punishments, at the same times, from the same teachers, and yet nothing seems to change. Where our aim is to help learners to develop self-regulation, we need them to understand that it really does matter *for them* how they choose to behave. We need to give them opportunities to have a try, make mistakes and rebound from their errors, in a safe and supportive environment. They need to understand that it will make their lives feel more useful, valuable and worthwhile if they manage to get better at self-regulating. When our learners leave our care, we want them to be out in society making good choices and feeling like they 'can do' the behaviours that will help them to be successful in their lives. Supporting a sense of agency will help them to achieve this.

Ideas about how much agency children can and should have vary. However, there has generally been a significant change in attitudes towards children's agency over the last century. In Western societies particularly, children now have much more of an opportunity to offer their opinions and talk about what it feels like to be a child. Researchers have noted that many modern parents view themselves and their children as equals who can discuss various issues with each other (Gurdal and Sorbring, 2018). The UN Convention on the Rights of the Child (see UNICEF, 2019) came into force in the UK in 1992. The Convention is the most widely ratified human rights treaty in the world. It has 54 articles detailing all aspects of a child's life and what their civil, political, economic, social and cultural rights should be. UNICEF's 'rights respecting schools' scheme (UNICEF, n.d.) encourages schools to create safe and inspiring places to learn that respect children's rights and agency.

The question of whether children are 'beings' or 'becomings' is central to how we conceptualise childhood and indeed to how we approach education (Uprichard, 2008). Are children 'adults in the making' or are they active agents in constructing their own lives? We can see this conceptualisation of children writ large in the talk about 'experts and novices' that has become prevalent in education debates in recent years. In this framing of education, adults are seen as 'experts' passing down the knowledge that they deem to be important; children are the 'novices' to whom that knowledge is delivered. However, ask a dinosaur-obsessed five-year-old to share their knowledge about dinosaurs and you will soon discover how much of an expert children can be, even at such a young age. When children come to us already speaking two or three languages, we need to have the humility to say that maybe we are not the experts in everything after all. When we think about learners as active agents, we grant them a mind of their own – we accept that they have their own will and should be given the chance to take control, make decisions and construct meaning for themselves. Their interests, ideas and inputs suddenly become much more important to our thinking around both pedagogy and curriculum.

Agency and trust

It is interesting to note that there is relatively little research into the role of agency within the education system (Mairitsch et al., 2023). Perhaps this is because the way in which the formal school system is set up presently mediates against our ability as educators to encourage and build agency. There is a constant pressure on schools and educators to push children and young people to meet ever-increasing expectations and demands and to ensure that they do their best in exams, but these goals are externally set and mediated. They are seen as a measure of 'success' for schools and also for teachers because we are effectively judged one against another as to who can get the 'best' results. There can be a high price to be paid by teachers who try to give learners space to fail – to refuse to intervene when a learner refuses to take responsibility for their own learning. It is a tricky balance to achieve, and over the years I have had many conversations with teachers who have felt pressured to over-support their learners, even when those learners did not seem to want to put in any work for themselves. Ironically, the best way in which to build attributes and attitudes such as responsibility, agency and a 'can do' attitude is to allow children and young people to have a go, to sometimes fail miserably but to keep trying. If your goal is self-regulation, there are perils in focusing on a perfect 'end result'.

In many ways, this is an issue of a lack of trust within the system. Politicians do not trust teachers or schools to 'do the right thing' for their learners, so they put in place accountability systems that use outputs as a measure of success. In turn, teachers and schools are less inclined to trust their learners because of the pressure to get a positive outcome for everyone. We see this lack of trust exemplified on social media in conversations around whether secondary schools in the UK should allow their learners to access the toilet when they need it. Something has broken in the relationship of trust between young people and the system when the assumption (and the reality for some schools) is that giving learners trust around going to the toilet is seen to be too much for either the schools or the young people to manage.

The idea of 'FAIL' being a 'first attempt in learning' has come to the fore in recent years, as people have realised the crucial role of failure in learning. If we are willing to take risks and give learning a go, we must also be willing to fail. When we learn how to cope with failure and to reflect on it to inform our next attempt at learning, we can move forwards and build resilience as well. A simple metaphor for this is the example of a child building a tower out of blocks. If they always stop at a 'safe' moment, when the tower is not particularly high or unstable, they might feel a sense of 'success'. However, if they can cope with going a little bit too far – of pushing outside their comfort zone – then they will build their tower higher and are likely to learn more about how to make it stable in the future. Being able to handle the tower crashing down – to effectively 'fail' at the task – is the best way in which to move forwards with their learning.

Agency and schools

The amount of agency that children and young people are given in the school system is often limited. Although some settings bring in strategies to try to enhance this aspect and allow learners to feel like they have a voice, the truth is that adults typically end up making most of the decisions. Clearly, this is partly about the realities of managing a situation where there are lots of children and young people and not as many adults. In addition, we cannot necessarily assume that our learners would always make sensible choices or even choose to focus on doing the same things if we asked them. It would also be hard to come to clear decisions in a school context if learners were consulted before any choices were made.

However, having worked in both schools and Early Years settings, there is certainly much that the school system might usefully learn from the approach to agency and autonomy that we typically see in the Early Years. Clearly, there are very different pressures between Early Years settings and school-based settings. However, with an increase in opportunities for young people to learn outside of the school system and an increase in young people taking this option, as shown in the rapidly dropping school attendance figures, it feels like one of the most pressing questions of our time. Effectively, building agency is about working in partnership – seeing children, young people and their parents or carers as part of a learning community.

There can be pushback against learners having a voice in how schools are run. For example, conversations on social media about student panels helping to interview teachers show how sensitive people are about this idea. Some educators appear dismissive of the young people whom they are applying to teach, suggesting that they cannot be trusted to make good decisions or that their decisions will be based on poor reasoning. While we accept that 'practice makes perfect' in all other areas of the curriculum, there is a sensitivity to allowing children and young people to be active in and, consequently, to practise decision-making. It is hard to give children agency, especially given the way in which our education system currently works, but it is also hard to see how children can learn to be responsible, active agents in their own lives without adults helping them to practise it.

Effective goal setting

It is interesting to consider what makes something a 'goal' rather than just an aim. Generally, a goal is something that we have not achieved yet, that we plan to actively work to achieve and that is not likely to happen on its own. By their very nature, goals are things that we want to achieve but that we know we might find difficult to do. Having a goal usually means striving to achieve something that we have not achieved before. When considering the difficulty of the goals that we set ourselves, it is useful to remember that there are different types of goals. Some goals are familiar, easy and do not require much in the way of skill or knowledge. Other goals are much more complex and might require learning or doing something new. To achieve what we might call these 'higher-order' goals, we need to apply the various executive functions that have been described in this book – we need to focus, pay attention, control our impulses and use our working memories.

Goal-setting theory (Locke and Latham, 1990) suggests that setting ourselves goals can promote us to feel more motivated and to learn more effectively. However, the effects of goal setting will depend on the properties of the goals that we set ourselves – some approaches work better than others. It is much less effective to just say 'try your hardest' or 'do your best' than to be specific about what we want to achieve. Similarly, where goals are seen as being too easy or far too difficult, this can impact motivation as well.

To work best, goals need to:

- ✓ give specific standards for performance
- ✓ be close at hand
- ✓ be seen as difficult but attainable.

When thinking about goals in a classroom context, this translates to teachers giving clarity of objectives, clear timings and targets, and plenty of challenge (with scaffolding as appropriate). We can support our learners by teaching them strategies to work towards their goals and helping them understand how to assess their progress towards a goal that they have set for themselves. When learners believe that they are learning a useful strategy, they feel greater control over their learning and feel more able to improve their skills. When an individual adopts a goal for themselves, they will feel more of a sense of efficacy if they attain it. In other words, effective goal setting is linked to self-efficacy and agency – the belief that we can perform at a specific level.

Interestingly, play is one of the most useful ways in which we can support children to set themselves goals and to create and handle challenges. Play promotes autonomy because it begins with the child. It can also work within the zone of proximal development because the child will stretch themselves, but within their understanding of their own limits. When playing, children set themselves goals or challenges and gradually learn how to cope if they do not reach them. Because play is generally felt to be a low-threat activity, children are unlikely to feel as much pressure to 'perform' as they would during academic tasks. Allowing learners of all ages to be playful in our classrooms is likely to support their ability to set themselves goals, work as active agents, deal with challenges and bounce back from difficulties.

The role of resilience

Resilience is an interesting word, and can evoke strong reactions from people. While we all want our learners to *be* resilient, for some children the simple act of turning up at school each day demonstrates a lot more resilience than we see from some adults. Resilience is about being able to cope with challenges and bounce back from failures without struggling, failing to cope or becoming emotionally dysregulated. Peer group interactions can support the development of resilience because of the social communication and negotiations that are involved. Children and young people learn that they can make friends, fall out and make friends again, and that the world continues to turn. This may be one of the reasons why the loss of peer interactions during the pandemic appears to have had such a negative impact on social communication skills for our learners.

There is much research to suggest that self-regulation skills are vital in supporting resilience – developing tenacity and the ability to cope with mistakes supports learners to be more resilient (Artuch-Garde et al., 2017; Gomez-Baya et al., 2020). When learners are self-regulated, their brains release chemicals such as dopamine, serotonin and endorphins, which help calm and organise the brain and enable them to think logically and rationally. In turn, learners are more likely to feel safe in a classroom setting because they are successful learners. The concept of 'grit' is closely linked to that of resilience – the ability to persevere to achieve long-term goals, which again links back to the idea of deferred gratification. Building self-regulation skills will help our learners build this grit and bounce back from challenges and failures in a complex and uncertain world. Those young people who arrive in our classrooms already subject to adverse stressors will find it more difficult than their peers to maintain a calm and resilient state. It is vital that adults offer them a model of what it looks like to stay calm in difficult situations.

Practical strategies for the classroom

Perhaps the best way in which to support and develop agency in your classroom is to think about all the ways in which you can hand over aspects of the classroom environment to the learners and enable them to make decisions. The idea is to send them the message that it is *their* classroom and *their* learning as much as it is *yours*. This means being willing to do something that many teachers (including me) find difficult – handing over the reins to the learners and letting them do more of the work than you. If you have ever found yourself standing at the front of the room, going 'Come back to me! Come back to me!' in an increasingly stressed and nervous voice, then I would recommend that you consider ways in which to situate the responsibility for *coming back to you* in the learners, rather than in you as their teacher.

A key strategy is to *ask* your learners questions about what works for them, rather than assuming that only you (or the school systems) can possibly make that choice. Human beings are naturally very heavily invested in making sure that things work for them personally. It is all about trying to hand over as much responsibility for the day-to-day management and decision-making of the classroom to the learners as possible, tapping into what really motivates them and makes them take responsibility for their own learning. There are plenty of ways in which you can do this, and many of these approaches will also help you to lower your workload:

- ✓ A good example of where you might hand over control is in the mismatch between many school reward systems and what children and young people are *motivated by* as a reward. Although consequences generally need to be consistent within a behaviour system, the same is not true of rewards, where there is greater scope for creativity. Your learners are far more likely to know what will motivate them than you are, so ask them for feedback and act on the most useful-sounding and appropriate strategies.
- ✓ We naturally hand over control when we ask for volunteers – for example, to hand things out or collect them in. Consider all the areas of your daily routine where someone else (the learners) can do the work. For example, in our setting, the learners chop up snacks for each other, as well as making choices about which foods they would like to eat when these are served. Obviously, there are multiple times in the school day when something needs handing out or collecting, such as registers, books, equipment and so on.
- ✓ Where you use a classroom-management strategy to gain the learners' attention, consider whether you can hand it over to the learners themselves to manage it. For example, if you commonly ring a bell or make some other kind of noise to bring the class back to you, what is to stop you from putting that responsibility in the hands of your learners? As mentioned previously, in our setting, one of the children rings a small handbell to bring the group together at the start of the day for circle time. Not only do the children respond immediately to their peers, but they also love the opportunity to take responsibility for ringing the bell.
- ✓ Where you can use a strategy that not only puts the responsibility in the hands of the class, but also actively makes it quite difficult to achieve, this pushes up the sense of trust, personal responsibility and agency – for example, saying to a class that you want them to stop working and return to you when the clock says a specific time, but that you are not going to give them a signal or any kind of indicator when this time arrives.

By having really high expectations of what your learners can manage and supporting them in various ways to achieve those things, you will give them the sense that it is worth utilising the agency that you have handed over to them. In turn, where this makes a genuine difference to their experience of school, they start to see that agency and goal-setting behaviours are of real value to them.

How not to be a helicopter

Ironically, one of the key roles of the teacher in helping learners work towards their goals and maintain their agency is the ability to step back and actively avoid interfering. Although we might offer scaffolds and supports, we are saying to the learner, 'You can do this for yourself.' This allows the child or young person sufficient space to feel a sense of agency, to encounter difficulty and challenge and, in doing so, to learn that they can not only cope with it but probably find a solution to it as well. When I am working with teachers, I describe this by saying, 'Don't be a helicopter.' Do not hover over children and young people because although this might make you feel like you are giving your input and support, it can often result in you simply getting in the way of the young person utilising their agency to resolve the problems for themselves.

It is worth reflecting on when and why you might be tempted to 'helicopter' – typically this is where you feel a pressure of some sort on yourself. For instance, the pressure to 'get through' the curriculum in the run-up to external exams might make you rush learners to settle, rather than encouraging them to manage the attentional control required for themselves. The pressure to 'keep the noise down' for the class next door might lead you to over-intervene when the class is getting noisy because of a worry about what others might think.

An interesting comment that I sometimes hear from educators, particularly those working with children in more advantaged situations, is about how some parents 'helicopter' over their children. In other words, these caregivers structure, over-help and over-schedule their children. Outside of school, every minute is filled in their diaries. Children will be taking violin lessons, doing ballet classes, going to Scouts/Guides, attending playdates and so on, with almost no time for them to make choices and decisions of their own. These parents may also be the ones who over-help with homework – ironically, the desire for their child to be seen to 'do well' mitigates the sense of agency that will help the child to self-regulate and build agency.

As with many things in teaching – and in this book – the first step is to reflect on your own beliefs and behaviours to best help your learners. What do I as a teacher need to do – or not do – to encourage a stronger sense of agency in my class?

- ✓ Be aware of the times and places where you are most likely to 'helicopter', due to your existing beliefs or concerns about learner behaviours or external pressures. For instance, in primary schools, this is often noticeable in the playground, where supervisory staff are nervous that children might hurt themselves and consequently tend to interject with commands such as 'Be careful!' or 'Don't fall!'. In a secondary school, we might see this in contexts where large numbers of learners are together in a social context, such as during lunchtime.

- ✓ Plan for challenge, risk-assess the environment, but remember to let children make the mistakes that they need to make to learn. There is always a tricky balance to be achieved between managing risk and supporting learners to manage their own risks.
- ✓ When you do need to intervene to support or warn a learner, describe what the child or young person can do in terms of taking a more active, agentic approach – for example, saying to a child 'Ah, I noticed you've made a bit of an error there in your maths, but I'm sure you can find it and fix it by yourself.'
- ✓ If you are concerned that this might mean that your learners feel abandoned or that they might panic if you ask them to do this by themselves, you can always scaffold these 'hands-off' approaches for the learner. Say to them, 'I'll come back and check how you're getting on in a few minutes' or set a timer and promise to come back once it runs out.
- ✓ Praise agency over attainment to help learners understand that they need to choose to put effort into their work to succeed, rather than being naturally 'talented' or, indeed, 'not talented' at something.
- ✓ Avoid praising outcomes ('That's a fantastic essay') and focus on praising agency, approach and effort ('I really liked the way you reworked that section'/'I really appreciate how you kept going when you were struggling with that concept'). This idea ties in closely with research into growth mindset from American psychologist Carol Dweck (see Further Reading).

Teachers often ask me for advice on handling what we might call 'pointless' or 'silly' questions from learners, as discussed at the end of Chapter 5 (see pages 75–77). It is interesting to consider *why* our learners might be in the habit of doing this, and it would be hard not to conclude that perhaps our habit of over-helping might be at least partly to blame. It is useful to consider how we feel about learners who want to please us – if we are honest, it can feel rather lovely when they want to do their best for us. Unfortunately, this sends the wrong message about self-regulated, independent approaches to learning. We need to support learners to understand that it is *themselves* that they should want to please, rather than us.

How to support agency

As well as thinking about your own tendency to over-help, there are lots of strategies that you can utilise to demonstrate, scaffold and model what 'being an active agent in my own learning' looks like. As with all aspects of learning, one of the keys to getting any approach in place is to model it for your learners yourself. This means not only expecting your learners to take risks and cope with failure, but showing yourself taking risks and coping with failures too. It is a tricky balance in the current climate in education to approach our classroom practice in this way, but in the end, we need to ask ourselves whom we are doing this for. If the answer is 'for the learners' rather than 'for Ofsted' (or whichever body holds you accountable), then we need to demonstrate courage and stick to our principles. Supporting agency is essentially about offering opportunities to make decisions, take responsibility and incorporate aspects of learners' interests and wishes into the curriculum. In order to build learner agency, you will need to be responsive and take some risks, as in the strategies given below:

- ✓ Offer your trust, especially to the hardest-to-trust learners. We cannot earn someone's trust if they never give it to us in the first place. Again, be ready for your learners to sometimes fail, and try not to see this as a reason not to take risks and give them challenges to cope with. When I talk with teachers about this, they will usually describe children as being far more trustworthy than they might have expected when given responsibility. Young people seem to rise to the challenge of being given trust, perhaps because it implies that you are putting your faith in what they can achieve.

- ✓ Ask learners about what they want and need, aiming to be responsive to their wishes within the bounds of professional responsibility. For example, teachers often find that school rewards stop working (or never 'work' in the first place) because the learners simply are not motivated by what is being offered. If you ask your learners what rewards would motivate them, you may find that they offer you a creative solution that works perfectly.

- ✓ A teacher once told me that she had done this and the class had said that their perfect reward was to watch a YouTube channel called *Man versus Food*. By promising them five minutes watching this eating competition channel in return for working really hard for 55 minutes of the lesson, she was able to remotivate a tricky low-attaining set.

- ✓ Appreciate your learners' interests and goals and aim to incorporate these in small and creative ways into your lessons. This does not mean making an entire topic or term's work about a specific learner's interest; it can simply involve dropping in a reference (for instance, as an analogy) or using some language that links to the area of interest. For example, if your class was obsessed with *The Great British Bake Off* you could call one of the tasks in your lesson 'The Showstopper'.

- ✓ Demonstrate to your learners that learning can happen outside and beyond the classroom. Give them opportunities to share learning that they have done through their own agency and volition. Talk about yourself as a learner and the choices that you have made during your life – both the positives and the negatives. Telling your classes what you failed at is probably more instructive than letting them know how you succeeded.

- ✓ Be open to feedback from the learners' perspectives about what works for them in terms of your approaches to teaching and learning. Consider offering them a selection of choices within lessons where appropriate, rather than always controlling everything yourself. For example, you could ask them to choose between using one format and another when doing a writing task.
- ✓ Be very clear that you are going to prioritise supportive peer relationships. Insist that learners do not talk over each other – if someone is addressing the class and a peer starts to talk over them, ask the individual to pause and to wait 'until the entire class is silent and listening to you'. There is no need to focus on what others are doing wrong; simply focus on the learner who is waiting to speak to reinforce what you want to see done right.
- ✓ Know your learners as individuals as far as possible, and how much support/pushing they are likely to need from you. This will vary from learner to learner, with some much more able to be self-starters and others needing reminders and a bit of coaching/nagging from the teacher.
- ✓ Encourage your learners to actively reflect on their own approaches to learning and why they were or were not successful. Explain concepts such as growth mindset to them, encouraging them to understand that it is effort rather than aptitude that matters most.
- ✓ Build on individual learner interests simply by demonstrating an interest in their chosen topic. This might mean bringing in a book that you know they will enjoy reading on a topic by which they are fascinated, or asking after them to find out how they got on in a sports match that they were playing at the weekend.

At all times, it is important for us to balance high expectations with realistic goals. Our learners need to feel successful but also to know that we believe they can strive for and achieve the best. When a learner repeatedly tries to succeed at something but finds it too difficult and subsequently fails, this can make them feel that there is something about them that is causing their failure, and consequently, their sense of agency may feel threatened. Again, scaffolding and ensuring appropriate levels of challenge are key. My book *The Ultimate Guide to Adaptive Teaching* (Bloomsbury) offers lots more ideas about how you can do this.

It is useful also to note the role of collective agency in self-regulation. Research suggests that where learners perceive the class or group as being supportive, this can foster motivation and a shared sense of responsibility (Mairitsch et al., 2023). Teachers can foster this sense of collective agency by paying attention to the group dynamics in a class and by learning from their colleagues. The teachers' collective approach to agency helps to determine the agency felt by the entire group. In an educational context, self-regulation happens within a social relationship, and by combining our shared knowledge, skills, resources and values, we can use agency to help shape the quality of our collective environment.

Agency and sustained shared thinking

One of the keys to developing self-regulation and feeling like active agents in our lives is our ability to think things through. We need to be able to create an internal monologue in which we consider goals – thinking about the best way in which to achieve them – coach and coax ourselves when things get difficult and reflect on our success or otherwise in attaining those goals. In a school context, adults can support children and young people to learn how to do this through a process called 'sustained shared thinking'. Talking ideas and thoughts through with a teacher or other significant adult, and building on these together in an open-ended exchange of ideas, can support children and young people in learning how to manage their own thoughts and behaviours as active agents in their own lives.

The technique known as sustained shared thinking is very similar to approaches such as Socratic questioning, where people work together to build a shared understanding through using open-ended questions. It can involve various forms of communication designed to draw out and build on each other's ideas. Some potential open-ended questions are given below:

- ✓ Clarifying: 'So you think that…'
- ✓ Suggesting: 'How about if we tried…?'
- ✓ Elaborating: 'Interesting, can you tell me more…?'
- ✓ Recapping: 'So, you began with this, now could you…'
- ✓ Referencing experiences: 'I remember when I…'
- ✓ Reminding: 'Don't forget that previously you…'
- ✓ Speculating: 'I wonder what would happen if…?'
- ✓ Encouraging: 'You worked so hard on that, now could you…?'
- ✓ Identifying alternative views: 'Let's imagine we are X, what might we do…?'

Supporting goal-setting behaviours

To maintain their motivation, learners need to believe that if they can change their behaviour, then they will get better outcomes. They also need to value the outcomes towards which they are working, and they need to believe that they can change their current approach. Where these factors all come together, learners have a high sense of self-efficacy and are likely to attain well. Clearly, one of the end goals of the school system is success in examinations. To support your learners' approach to this, give them key strategies for success, such as:

- ✓ learning techniques to avoid procrastination – for example, setting yourself a deadline and avoiding distractions
- ✓ creating checklists to stay on track and give themselves a sense of success
- ✓ understanding why it is useful to break down information that they are revising into small chunks to make it easier to handle and remember
- ✓ using key strategies for memorising information, such as reframing it, self-quizzing and creating mnemonics
- ✓ understanding how to pass exams, including the importance of marks, mark schemes and sticking to timings.

Although the concept comes more from the world of business than education, SMART targets are a very useful way of helping learners conceptualise effective goal-setting behaviours. These are targets that are:

- Specific
- Measurable
- Achievable
- Relevant
- Time-bound.

Work through some examples with exam-age learners to show them how to set these kinds of targets.

Modelling failure

If we want to support our learners to become more resilient, we need to show them what it looks like to cope well with failure. A common concern expressed to me by the teachers I meet is that some learners go into a complete emotional meltdown when something goes wrong or when they make a mistake. We need to show learners a clear example of 'coping with failure' so that they can learn from the model that we provide. It is an interesting experience for educators to model failure, though, because our roles require us to be seen as a 'font of all knowledge'. If we are honest, we can tend to set ourselves up as 'the expert', which, in turn, can make it more difficult to admit when we get something wrong. Of course, teachers are only human, just like their learners, and the act of modelling failure is a crucial part of supporting your learners to develop self-regulation. Here are some thoughts about how you can do just that:

- ✓ Show a model of failing well: say sorry when you make a mistake.
- ✓ Make deliberate mistakes, such as spelling errors, and ask your learners to spot them and tell you what your error is.

- ✓ Do not give into the urge to immediately 'repair' errors for learners – encourage them to find and repair the mistakes for themselves.
- ✓ Create an environment where learners are encouraged to 'brag' about their errors because of the way in which they help with learning. Some schools have 'Failure Fridays', where mistakes are celebrated throughout the setting.
- ✓ Do fast activities and make it clear that part of learning is understanding that you can experiment, try something quickly and decide to throw it away once you are done.

Conclusion

In many ways, self-regulation and self-regulated learning skills are the ultimate goal of 'an education' because they allow children and young people to become learners for the long term, and not just while they are in our classrooms. When children and young people learn to be self-regulated, their education goes beyond what they learn at school and the exams that they pass because learning in all its forms becomes a lifelong pursuit. Self-regulation skills allow our learners to make their way beyond the school gates as kind, caring, valuable and valued members of society. They know how to have empathy, how best to behave towards others, how to manage their emotions, how to build positive relationships, how to communicate socially and how to focus on the right things at the right times. Even when their teachers are no longer in the room, our influence lives on through the behavioural and learning skills that we have taught them.

To complete this book, I would like to share a proud personal story about my own child and how being self-regulated in both behaviour and learning can enable amazing achievements. During the pandemic, when schools were closed and lockdowns were in progress, our youngest decided to start learning Japanese. Obviously, there were no in-person lessons available, but with the help of YouTube, the internet, some kanji books and a lot of hard work and dedication, they somehow managed to learn Japanese alongside online school lessons. On the return to school, I asked whether it would be possible for them to sit a GCSE in Japanese since so much work had gone into learning it. The school very kindly facilitated this and the result was a grade 9, purely through self-study! The next step was an exam called the Japanese Language Proficiency Test, which is usually taken by people planning to spend time studying or working in Japan. When our child achieved JLPT Level 2, scoring in the top three per cent in the world (again, entirely through self-study), we were impressed and delighted. To top it all off, they have just secured a place at Oxford University to study Japanese: now *that* is proof of the incredible power of self-regulation.

My stated goal at the start of this book was to think about how we can build an approach that supports 'learning to behave' – one that embeds self-regulation into the daily lives of our schools, helping all our learners to become better self-regulated. I hope that you have found this book to be a useful introduction to and overview of the subject – what self-regulation is, why it is important and how it develops. I also hope that you have come away with plenty of practical ideas about what you can do to help children and young people learn to behave. As educators, a key goal of our work is to help them understand 'how to behave' in the widest possible sense, so that children and young people learn to participate in society as fully-rounded individuals. I hope that this book will succeed in helping you to achieve just that.

Further Reading

Center for Self-Determination Theory, 'Theory', https://selfdeterminationtheory.org/theory
Center on the Developing Child, Harvard University, https://developingchild.harvard.edu
Dweck, C. (2017), *Mindset – Updated Edition: Changing the Way You think to Fulfil Your Potential*. London: Robinson.
O'Regan, F. (2018), 'Teaching and managing students with ADHD: Systems, strategies, solutions', Shire Pharmaceuticals, www.adhdfoundation.org.uk/wp-content/uploads/2022/03/Teaching-and-Managing-Students-with-ADHD.pdf
Price, C. J. and Hooven, C. (2018), 'Interoceptive awareness skills for emotion regulation: Theory and approach of Mindful Awareness in Body-oriented Therapy (MABT)', *Frontiers in Psychology*, 9, 798.
The MEHRIT Centre, 'Self-reg resource library', https://self-reg.ca/resource-library

References

These references are research and interesting articles that link to the points made and topics explored in this book. I have tried wherever possible throughout the book to refer to pieces of research that are published for open access on the internet, rather than those where you will need to pay to access the full studies. However, in some instances, you will only be able to read the abstract/summary of the research, rather than the full paper. In addition, you will find references to some more generalist articles referenced in the book, which give an overview of different aspects of self-regulation. Please note: Where possible, I have chosen links to organisations that are likely to maintain their research presence online. However, the nature of the internet means that some of these links might expire over time.

Aldiebears Adventures (2023), 'Aldie and Mama's bedtime conversation', www.youtube.com/watch?v=AJZj1NINxms

Artuch-Garde, R., González-Torres, M. d. C., de la Fuente, J., Vera, M. M., Fernández-Cabezas, M. and López-García, M. (2017), 'Relationship between resilience and self-regulation: A study of Spanish youth at risk of social exclusion', *Frontiers in Psychology*, 8, 612.

Baer, R. A., Smith, G. T., Hopkins, J., Krietemeyer, J. and Toney, L. (2006), 'Using self-report assessment methods to explore facets of mindfulness', *Assessment*, 13, (1), 27–45.

Bandura, A. (1991), 'Social cognitive theory of self-regulation', *Organizational Behavior and Human Decision Processes*, 50, (2), 248–87.

Barker, J. E., Semenov, A. D., Michaelson, L., Provan, L. S., Snyder, H. S. and Munakata, Y. (2014), 'Less-structured time in children's daily lives predicts self-directed executive functioning', *Frontiers in Psychology*, 5, 593.

Barragan, R. C., Brroks, R. and Meltzoff, A. N. (2020), 'Altruistic food sharing behavior by human infants after a hunger manipulation', *Scientific Reports*, 10, 1785.

Batson, D. and Ahmad, N. Y. (2009), 'Using empathy to improve intergroup attitudes and relations', *Social Issues and Policy Review*, 3, (1), 141–77.

Battich, L., Fairhurst, M. and Deroy, O. (2020), 'Coordinating attention requires coordinated senses', *Psychonomic Bulletin & Review*, 27, 1126–38.

Berkman, E. T., Graham, A. M. and Fisher, P. A. (2012), 'Training self-control: A domain-general translational neuroscience approach', *Child Development Perspectives*, 6, (4), 374–84.

Carlo, G., White, R. M. B., Streit, C., Knight, G. P. and Zeiders, K. H. (2017), 'Longitudinal relations among parenting styles, prosocial behaviors, and academic outcomes in U.S. Mexican adolescents', *Child Development*, 89, (2), 577–92.

Center for Self-Determination Theory (CSDT) (2024), 'Applying self-determination theory to education', https://selfdeterminationtheory.org/topics/application-education

Center on the Developing Child (n.d.), 'Executive function & self-regulation', https://developingchild.harvard.edu/science/key-concepts/executive-function

Center on the Developing Child (2011), 'Building the brain's "air traffic control" system: How early experiences shape the development of executive function', Working paper 11, https://developingchild.harvard.edu/wp-content/uploads/2011/05/How-Early-Experiences-Shape-the-Development-of-Executive-Function.pdf

Chang, H., Shaw, D. S. and Cheong, JW. (2015), 'The development of emotional and behavioral control in early childhood: Heterotypic continuity and relations to early school adjustment', *Journal of Child and Adolescent Behavior*, 3, (3), 204.

Code, J. (2020), 'Agency for learning: Intention, motivation, self-efficacy and self-regulation', *Frontiers in Education*, 5, www.frontiersin.org/articles/10.3389/feduc.2020.00019/full

Cowley, S. (2024), *Getting Your Class to Behave* (6th edn). London: Bloomsbury.

Cutuli, D. (2014), 'Cognitive reappraisal and expressive suppression strategies role in the emotion regulation: An overview on their modulatory effects and neural correlates', *Frontiers in Systems Neuroscience*, 8, 175.

Duckworth, A. L., Gendler, T. S. and Gross, J. J. (2016), 'Situational strategies for self-control', *Perspectives on Psychological Science*, 11, (1), 35–55.

Education Endowment Foundation (EEF) (2021), 'Metacognition and self-regulation', https://educationendowmentfoundation.org.uk/education-evidence/teaching-learning-toolkit/metacognition-and-self-regulation

Education Endowment Foundation (EEF) (2023), 'Self-regulation strategies', https://educationendowmentfoundation.org.uk/education-evidence/early-years-toolkit/self-regulation-strategies

Firth, P. (2015), 'Wired for empathy: How and why stories cultivate emotions', Firesteel, http://firesteelwa.org/2015/07/wired-for-empathy-how-and-why-stories-cultivate-emotions

Frith, C. and Frith, U. (2005), 'Theory of mind', *Current Biology*, 15, (17), R644.

Geangu, E., Benga, O., Stahl, D. and Striano, T. (2010), 'Contagious crying beyond the first days of life', *Infant Behaviour and Development*, 33, (3), 279–88.

Gomez-Baya, D., Tomé, G., Reis, M. and Gaspar de Matos, M. (2020), 'Long-term self-regulation moderates the role of internal resources for resilience in positive youth development in Portugal', *The Journal of Genetic Psychology*, 181, (2–3), 127–49.

Gross, J. J. and John, O. P. (2003), 'Individual differences in two emotion regulation processes: Implications for affect, relationships, and well-being', *Journal of Personality and Social Psychology*, 85, (2), 348–362.

Grossmann, T., Oberecker, R., Koch, S. P. and Friederici, A. D. (2010), 'The developmental origins of voice processing in the human brain', *Neuron*, 65, (6), 852–8.

Gurdal, S. and Sorbring, E. (2018), 'Children's agency in parent–child, teacher–pupil and peer relationship contexts', *International Journal of Qualitative Studies on Health and Well-being*, 13, (Suppl 1), 1565239.

Hawker, L. (2021), '"Slant" won't work for SEND students, so what does?', ADHD Foundation, www.adhdfoundation.org.uk/2021/09/13/slant-wont-work-for-send-students-so-what-does

Henriques, M. (2019), 'Can the legacy of trauma be passed down the generations?', BBC Future, www.bbc.com/future/article/20190326-what-is-epigenetics

Katz, P. and Zalk, S. (1978) 'Modification of children's racial attitudes', *Developmental Psychology*, 14(5), pp. 447–461. doi:10.1037/0012-1649.14.5.447.

Klossek, U. M. H., Russell, J. and Dickinson, A. (2008), 'The control of instrumental action following outcome devaluation in young children aged between 1 and 4 years', *Journal of Experimental Psychology: General*, 137, (1), 39–51.

Köhler-Dauner, F., Order, E., Gulde, M., Mayer, I., Fegert, J. M., Ziegenhain, U. and Waller, C. (2022), 'Maternal sensitivity modulates child's parasympathetic mode and buffers sympathetic activity in a free play situation', *Frontiers in Psychology*, 13, 868848.

Korkmaz, B. (2011), 'Theory of mind and neurodevelopmental disorders of childhood', *Pediatric Research*, 69, 101–8.

Kross, E. and Ayduk, O. (2016), 'Self-distancing: Theory, research, and current directions', *Advances in Experimental Social Psychology*, 55, 81–136.

Kucirkova, N. (2019), 'How could children's storybooks promote empathy? A conceptual framework based on developmental psychology and literary theory', *Frontiers in Psychology*, 10, 121.

Le Courtois, S. (n.d.), 'The Dark Side of rewards and punishments in the classroom part I', Chartered College of Teaching Research Hub, https://my.chartered.college/research-hub/the-dark-side-of-rewards-and-punishments-in-the-classroom-part-i

Lemov, D. (2023), 'Tracking in classrooms: What I really think (and wrote)', *Teach Like a Champion*, Doug Lemov's Field Notes, https://teachlikeachampion.org/blog/tracking-in-classrooms-what-i-really-think-and-wrote

Levy, J., Goldstein, A. and Feldman, R. (2019), 'The neural development of empathy is sensitive to caregiving and early trauma', *Nature Communications*, 10, 1905.

Locke, E. A. and Latham, G. P. (1990), *A Theory of Goal Setting & Task Performance*. Upper Saddle River, NJ: Prentice-Hall.

Mairitsch, A., Sulis, G., Mercer, S. and Bauer, D. (2023), 'Putting the social into learner agency: Understanding social relationships and affordances', *International Journal of Educational Research*, 120, 102214.

Manyukhina, Y. and Wyse, D. (2021), 'Children's agency: What is it, and what should be done?', *BERA Blog*, www.bera.ac.uk/blog/childrens-agency-what-is-it-and-what-should-be-done

Mauss, I. B., Bunge, S. A. and Gross, J. J. (2007), 'Automatic emotion regulation', *Social and Personality Psychology Compass*, 1, (1), 146–67.

Mischel, W. (2014) 'The marshmallow test: Mastering self-control', *Scientific American*, 311(3), doi:10.1038/scientificamerican0914-92c.

Mischel, W. and Ebbesen, E. B. (1970), 'Attention in delay of gratification', *Journal of Personality and Social Psychology*, 16, (2), 329–37.

Montroy, J. J., Bowles, R. P., Skibbe, L. E., McClelland, M. M. and Morrison, F. J. (2016), 'The development of self-regulation across early childhood', *Developmental Psychology*, 52, (11), 1744–62.

Muijs, D. and Bokhove, C. (2020), 'Metacognition and self-regulation: Evidence review', Education Endowment Foundation, https://d2tic4wvo1iusb.cloudfront.net/production/documents/guidance/Metacognition_and_self-regulation_review.pdf?v=1718011711

Murray, D. W. and Hamoudi, A. (2016), 'A brief on self-regulation and toxic stress: How do acute and chronic stress impact the development of self-regulation?', U.S. Department of Health and Human Services, www.acf.hhs.gov/sites/default/files/documents/opre/6_brainlogo_508.pdf

Murray, L., Halligan, S. and Cooper, P. (2019), 'Postnatal depression and young children's development', in C. H. Zeanah (ed.), *Handbook of Infant Mental Health* (4th edn). New York: The Guilford Press, pp. 175–86.

Obradović, J., Sulik, M. J. and Shaffer, A. (2021), 'Learning to let go: Parental over-engagement predicts poorer self-regulation in kindergartners', *Journal of Family Psychology*, 35, (8), 1160–70.

Ofsted (2019), 'Education inspection framework: Overview of research', https://assets. publishing.service.gov.uk/media/6034be17d3bf7f265dbbe2ef/Research_for_EIF_ framework_updated_references_22_Feb_2021.pdf

O'Regan, F. (2018), 'Teaching and managing students with ADHD: Systems, strategies, solutions', Shire Pharmaceuticals, www.adhdfoundation.org.uk/wp-content/uplo ads/2022/03/Teaching-and-Managing-Students-with-ADHD.pdf

Panadero, E. (2017), 'A review of self-regulated learning: Six models and four directions for research', *Frontiers in Psychology*, 8, 422.

Paulmann, S. and Weinstein, N. (2023), 'Teachers' motivational prosody: A pre-registered experimental test of children's reactions to tone of voice used by teachers', *British Journal of Educational Psychology*, 93, (2), 437–52.

Perry, B. D. (n.d.), 'The Neurosequential Network', www.neurosequential.com

Perry, B. D. (2024), 'Handouts', www.bdperry.com/handouts

Šimić, G., Tkalčić, M., Vukić, V., Mulc, D., Španić, E., Šagud, M., Olucha-Bordonau, F. E., Vukšić, M. and Hof, P. R. (2021), 'Understanding emotions: Origins and roles of the amygdala', *Biomolecules*, 11, (6), 823.

Siraj-Blatchford, I. (2009), 'Conceptualising progression in the pedagogy of play and sustained shared thinking in early childhood education: A Vygotskian perspective', *Education and Child Psychology*, 26, (2), 77–89.

Sloan, A. T., Jones, N. A. and Scott Kelso, J. A. (2023), 'Meaning from movement and stillness: Signatures of coordination dynamics reveal infant agency', *Proceedings of the National Academy of Sciences*, 120, (39), e2306732120.

Sørensen, L., Osnes, B., Visted, E., Lillebostad Svendsen, J., Adolfsdottir, S., Binder, P.-E. and Schanche, E. (2018), 'Dispositional mindfulness and attentional control: The specific association between the mindfulness facets of non-judgment and describing with flexibility of early operating orienting in conflict detection', *Frontiers in Psychology*, 9, 2359.

Sun, J., He, L., Chen, Q., Yang, W., Wei, D. and Qiu, J. (2022), 'The bright side and dark side of daydreaming predict creativity together through brain functional connectivity', *Human Brain Mapping*, 43, (3), 902–14.

Tarullo, A R., Obradović, J. and Gunnar, M. R. (2009), 'Self-control and the developing brain', *Zero to Three*, 29, (3), 31–7.

Twito, L., Israel, S., Simonson, I. and Knafo-Noam, A. (2019), 'The motivational aspect of children's delayed gratification: Values and decision making in middle childhood', *Frontiers in Psychology*, 10, 1649.

UNICEF (n.d.), 'Rights respecting schools: Creating safe and inspiring places to learn', www. unicef.org.uk/rights-respecting-schools

UNICEF (2019), 'How we protect children's rights with the UN Convention on the Rights of the Child', www.unicef.org.uk/what-we-do/un-convention-child-rights

Uprichard, E. (2008), 'Children as "being" and "becomings": Children, childhood and temporality', *Children & Society*, 22, (4), 303–13.

Vygotsky, L. S. (1978), *Mind in Society: The Development of Higher Psychological Processes*. Cambridge, MA: Harvard University Press.

White, R. E., Prager, E. O., Schaefer, C., Kross, E., Duckworth, A. L. and Carlson, S. M. (2017), 'The "Batman Effect": Improving perseverance in young children', *Child Development*, 88, (5), 1563–71.

Whitebread, D. and Basilio, M. (2012), 'The emergence and early development of self-regulation in young children', *Profesorado*, 16, (1), 15–33.

Woodward, A. L. (2009), 'Infants' grasp of others' intentions', *Current Directions in Psychological Science*, 18, (1), 53–7.

Yehuda, R. (2022), 'How parents' trauma leaves biological traces in children', *Scientific American*, www.scientificamerican.com/article/how-parents-rsquo-trauma-leaves-biological-traces-in-children

Index

acute stress 32
adverse childhood experiences 28, 30
    and emotional regulation 103, 104, 105
    and empathy development 119
    and impulse control 67
    and sense of self 101
agency 3, 13, 14, 27, 42, 86, 92, 93, 112, 129, 136
    avoiding interference 139–40
    balancing high expectations with realistic goals 142
    of children, attitudes towards 133
    collective 142–3
    conceptualising 131–3
    development of 130–1
    handing over control to learners 137–8
    and impulse control 68
    practical strategies for classroom 137–45
    and provision of choices to learners 54, 55
    and routines 53–4
    and school system 134–5
    and self-regulation development 29, 30
    sense of 132
    supporting 140–3
    and sustained shared thinking 143
    and trust 133–4
    see also goal setting
amygdala 67, 113
anterior cingulate cortex 66, 80
attachments
    and impulse control development 67
    of infants with carers 49
    issues, and emotional regulation 104
    with trusted adults 28–9
attentional control 9, 24–5, 73, 79–80
    attention of teachers 87–8
    concentrations and distractions 83–5
    development of 80–2
    and emotions 103
    and environment 89–93
    getting the attention of the class 88–9
    joint attention 82–3
    managing auditory inputs 92–3
    managing visuals 90–1
    and mindfulness 95–6
    practical strategies for classroom 86–96
    and SLANT 85–6
    strategies for directing and maintaining attention 93–5
Attention Autism 83
attention deficit disorder (ADD), learners with 74–5
attention deficit hyperactivity disorder (ADHD), learners with 74–5, 86, 104
attention deployment 71
auditory inputs, managing 92–3
autism, learners with 82, 86, 102, 104, 106, 120
automatic emotion regulation 103
autonomic nervous system 99, 104
autonomy 13, 14, 68, 95, 131, 135, 136

behavioural synchrony 98–9
behaviour(s) 1–3, 2, 20, 22–3
    as communication 35, 36–8
    definitions of 49–50
    as feedback 35, 36–8
    goal-oriented 26
    influence of proprioception on 51–2
    low-level misbehaviours 19, 24, 37, 49
    no excuses systems 3
    and person, separation between 55–6, 57
    poor/problematic 2, 23, 36, 37, 50, 51, 57–8, 76
    see also self-regulation
behaviours, managing

adapting curriculum provision 61–3
adapting routines/approaches 58–61
adapting triggers 63–4
development of behavioural control 48–9
focusing on positive 55, 87
practical strategies for classroom 54–64
pre-empting problematic behaviours 57–8, 76
routines 52–4
unconditional positive regard 30, 55–7, 127
whole-school systems 47, 48
board games 73
body map 51
brain 17, 25, 79, 112–13, 137
and attentional control development 80, 83
development 11, 27, 30, 31, 49, 50, 66, 81, 98
effects of stress on 32
and impulse control development 66–7
processes, involved in self-regulation 20–1
and proprioceptive input 51
reptilian 57
and routines 52
brain breaks 21, 50, 64, 111
breathing exercises 23, 43, 109

calm zones 109
'can do' attitude 27, 134
card games 73
challenges 16, 27, 68, 130
coping with 21, 22, 26, 29, 110, 136
and mental flexibility 21
and play 136
and scaffolding by teachers 112
and self-regulation development 29
choices, making 3, 30, 47, 53–4, 86, 129
chronic stress 32
cognitive change 71
cold calling 85
collective agency 142–3
colours, environment 91
communication, behaviour as 35
co-regulation 39–41
feedback 36–8

practical strategies for classroom 41–3
thinking things through 40, 41
concentration 24, 49, 79, 80, 83–5, 90
conscience alley 124
coping 8, 21, 27, 39–40, 65
with challenges 21, 22, 26, 29, 110, 136
with failure 21, 22, 26, 134, 140, 144
mechanisms 41
with sensory overload 82
with stress 32
co-regulation 11, 21, 23, 25, 27, 28, 36, 38–41, 42, 99
Covid-19 pandemic 2, 7, 137, 147
crying in infants 25, 27, 36, 48, 66, 118
curriculum 16, 133
provision, adapting 61–3
stories in 123

daydreaming 85
decibel meter 93
deferred gratification *see* delayed gratification
delayed gratification 21, 24, 65, 130, 137
and adverse childhood experiences 28
importance of 69
marshmallow experiment 12–13, 28–9, 30, 70, 71
and self-distancing 70
see also impulse control
distractions 25, 49, 75, 80, 82, 83–5, 87, 89–93, 94
drama warm-up activity 73

early childhood experiences
and emotional regulation 103, 104, 105
and impulse control 67
and self-regulation 27–8, 30
and sense of self 101
Education Endowment Foundation (EEF) 1, 8–9, 10
emotional attunement 98–9, 121, 125
emotional co-regulation 40
emotional literacy 106, 107
emotional meltdown 20, 39–40, 107, 144
emotional regulation 9, 14, 17, 20, 22, 25, 39–40, 42–3, 82, 83, 97–8
acknowledging and handling emotions 102–3

development of 98–9
emotions and learning 103–4
emotions check 109–10
identifying and exploring emotions 107
issues with 104
naming of emotions by learners 105
noticing and describing emotions 105–6
other sensory inputs 107–8
practical strategies for the
classroom 105–16
and prosody 112–14
role of interoception in feelings 100–1
role of teachers 111–12
scaffolding emotions 110–11
and sense of self 101–2
strategies for managing
emotions 108–9
supporting emotionally dysregulated
learners 114–16
of teachers 114
emotion thermometer 107
empathy 9, 22, 25, 98, 117–18
'caring for' activities 125–6
development of 9–10, 70, 118–19
and educators 120–1
grouping of learners 126
learning through narratives 121–4
modelling 124–5
positive trait attribution 126–7
practical strategies for the
classroom 123–7
and theory of mind 11, 12, 119–20
environment 23, 98, 132, 145
and agency 131
and attentional control 80, 81, 82,
83–4, 89–93
and impulse control 67, 74
and self-regulation development 27,
28, 29, 30
and stress response system 101
executive function 8, 12, 19, 20–1, 22,
83, 135
development of 11, 30
and overly structured activities 53
external regulation 14
extrinsic motivators 14–15, 18

facial expressions 31, 99, 106, 109, 118, 120
FAIL (first attempt in learning) 17, 71, 134

failure 17, 27, 68
coping with 21, 22, 26, 134, 140, 144
and learning 26
modelling 144–5
false beliefs 12, 119
feedback
behaviour as 35, 36–8
from learners 138, 142
fight or flight response 23, 39, 40, 99
flexible consistency 58
focus *see* attentional control

games, for impulse control
development 72–4
gender differences in self-regulation
development 68
genetics
and adverse childhood experiences 30
and impulse control 67
and trauma 104
gestures 31, 58, 74, 76
goal setting 21, 26, 27, 129, 130, 138
behaviours, development of 130–1
behaviours, supporting 143–4
effective 135–6
SMART (specific, measurable,
achievable, relevant, time-bound)
75, 144
see also agency
Grandmother's footsteps (game) 73
grit 137
growth mindset 26, 126, 140, 142

hearing
development in infants 80–1
impairment, learners with 88, 92
heavy work for proprioception
development 51
helicopter-type parenting style 29, 68

identified regulation 14
imaginative focus 50, 61
immersive story-reading 124
impulse control 9, 21, 23–4, 25, 30, 49, 50,
65–6, 93
cycle of 70–1
development of 66–7
handing over behaviours to learners 72
handling Q&A sessions 75–7

of learners with ADD/ADHD 74–5
marshmallow experiment 12–13, 28–9, 70, 71
practical strategies for classroom 72–7
self-control development 67–8
and self-distancing 69–70
sensation, learners knowing 72
strategies 71–2
and theory of mind 120
see also delayed gratification
infant development 27, 48–9
agency and goal-setting behaviours 130–1
attentional control 80–1
emotional regulation 98–9
empathy 118
impulse control 66
in-group/out-group identification 122
inhibitory control *see* impulse control
integrated regulation 14
interoception 14, 25, 99, 107
and emotional regulation 105–6, 107–8
role in feelings 100–1
intrinsic motivation 13, 14–15, 86, 95, 103–4
introjected regulation 14
involuntary attention 81

joint attention 82–3

labelling of learners, avoiding 56
language 127
noticing and describing emotions 105–6
role in empathy development 124–5
and self-regulation 11, 30–1, 41
lateral thinking 21, 57
learner interests 3, 104, 130, 141, 142
lighting, and attentional control 91

marshmallow experiment 12–13, 28–9, 30, 70, 71
Maslow's hierarchy of needs 14
meditation 70, 75, 95, 96
mental flexibility 21
metacognition 7, 8, 11, 14, 17, 42, 77, 86, 102, 115–16
mindfulness 13–14, 61, 70, 75, 95–6, 108–9
'minute to moan' activity 94
mirror neurons 39

modelling 33, 36, 42, 91, 92, 99, 111, 137, 140
for emotional regulation 115–16
of empathy 124–5
of failure 144–5
by parents/carers 49
of positive attitude 17
of self-calming strategies 39
motivation 2, 136
and agency 27
and collective agency 142
and emotions 103
extrinsic motivators 14–15, 18
intrinsic 13, 14–15, 86, 95, 103–4
practical approaches for 17–18
and school rewards 138, 141
self-determination theory 13–14
musical statues 72–3

narratives, empathy development through 121–4
no excuses systems 3
noise 92–3

orbitofrontal cortex 66

parasympathetic nervous system 99
parenting 119
emotionally attuned 98–9
helicopter-type 29, 68
and impulse control development 68
parents/carers
interplay of babies with 49
partnership with 32–3
role in attentional control development 81–2
role in emotional regulation development 98–9
role in empathy development 118, 124
self-soothing 39
'serve and return' interactions 31
peer relationships 18, 137, 142
play
and empathy development 118
and goal setting 136
and impulse control 72–4
and joint attention 82
pointless questions 76, 140
positive aspects, focusing on 55, 87

positive trait attribution 126–7
post-natal depression (PND) 31, 119
poverty 28, 67–8
prefrontal cortex 66, 68, 80
pretend play 118
problematic behaviours 2, 50, 57–8, 76
process model of self-control 70–1
proprioception 104
    and impulse control 72–3
    influence on classroom behaviour 51–2
prosody, and emotional regulation 112–14

Q&A sessions, handling 75–7
quiet critters 92–3

reading performance, and attention span 83
Ready ready (game) 73
reappraisal of emotions 102
reasonable adjustments 23, 50, 62, 63
repetitive activities 96
resilience 7, 26, 32, 136–7, 144
resonance 31
response modulation 72
restorative approaches to behaviour management 3
rewards 14–15, 18, 63, 138, 141
role models 123
role play 106, 118, 124
routines 52–3, 57
    adapting 58–61
    and agency 53–4

scaffolding-type co-regulation 40
school policies 2, 17, 20, 108
secret gestures 74
'secret student' technique 72
security, sense of 28–9, 40, 49, 52
selective attention 81
self-actualisation 14
self-control
    development of 67–8
    process model of 70–1
self-determination theory 13–14
self-distancing 9, 13, 69–70, 71, 122
self-efficacy 132, 136, 143
self-regulated learning 8, 9–10, 12, 26, 132, 147

self-regulation 1, 2, 7–8, 9, 12, 19–20, 22, 48, 132, 147
    attentional control 9, 24–5, 73, 79–96
    definition of 8–9, 16
    delayed gratification 12–13, 21, 24, 28–9, 30, 65, 69, 70, 71
    development of 10–11, 27–31, 68
    and early childhood experiences 27–8, 30
    emotional regulation 9, 17, 20, 22, 25, 39–40, 42–3, 97–116
    empathy 9–10, 22, 25, 70, 98, 117–27
    and executive function 20–1
    extrinsic motivators 14–15, 18
    goal-oriented behaviours, challenge and failure 26
    importance of 15–16
    impulse control 9, 21, 23–4, 25, 30, 49, 50, 65–77
    influence of stress on 31–2
    intrinsic motivators 14–15
    and language 11, 30–1, 41
    learner agency 27
    managing our behaviours 22–3
    marshmallow experiment 12–13, 28–9, 30, 70, 71
    practical strategies for classroom 16–18, 32–3
    and proprioceptive input 52
    self-determination theory 13–14
    see also agency; co-regulation; motivation
self-soothing 39, 99
SEND, learners with 52, 55, 62, 74, 81, 86, 91
sense of self 27, 42, 101–2, 126, 129
sensory overload 23, 50, 64, 82, 92
sensory processing 23, 80, 81, 82, 101
'serve and return' interactions 11, 30, 31, 98, 118
sight (sense), development in infants 81
silent signals 89
silent spot 88
'Simon says' (game) 73
situation modification 71
situation selection 71
SLANT 85–6
sleep disruption/deprivation 67–8

SMART goals 75, 144
smell, sense of 80, 84
snap (card game) 73
social cognitive theory 132
social communication 2, 8, 9, 15, 16, 66, 68, 82, 137
stories 121–4
storyboarding 124
stream of consciousness exercise 94–5
stress 30, 42, 50, 99
    impact on empathy development 119
    and impulse control 67
    influence on self-regulation 31–2
    and interoception 101
    predictable 32
    unpredictable 32
stress response system (SRS) 32, 101
suppression of emotions 102–3
sustained shared thinking 30, 143
sympathetic nervous system 99

talk/talking
    to learners 16, 17, 54, 56, 72, 86, 106, 108, 141
    'serve and return' interactions 11, 30, 31
    talk partners 76, 94
tantrums 40
taste, sense of 80
terrible twos 49
theory of mind 11–12, 119–20
'three before me' strategy 77
toddlers 25, 49, 65
Too Noisy (app) 93

touch, sense of 80
trauma 32, 50, 101, 104
trauma-informed approaches to behaviour management 3
triggers, avoiding 63–4
trust 125, 141
    and agency 133–4
    attachments with trusted adults 28–9
    and delayed gratification 69

unconditional positive regard 30, 55–7, 127
UN Convention on the Rights of the Child (UNICEF) 132

vagus nerve 99, 100
values-based education 120, 122
visual perspective taking 119
visual reminders 91
visuals, managing 90–1
voice of teachers 111, 112–14, 125
volcano breathing 109
voluntary attention 81
volunteering 138

What's the time Mr Wolf? (game) 73
whole-school initiatives for parents/carers 33
working memory 20–1, 41, 93
workshops for parents/carers 33

zero tolerance 3
zone of proximal development 39, 115, 136